C000185458

The Pony Club
Stoneleigh Park
Kenilworth
Warwickshire
CV8 2RW

Website: www.pcuk.org

*The Pony Club Guide to Endurance Riding*
is published by The Pony Club

British Library Cataloguing in Publication Data.
A catalogue record for this book is available from the British Library.

ISBN 978-1-907279-21-8

Design and Production: Paul G. Harding
www.hardingbooks.com

Printed by Halstan Printing Group in Amersham, UK
www.halstan.co.uk

**Trade distribution by Kenilworth Press**
**An imprint of Quiller Publishing Ltd.**
Wykey House, Wykey, Shrewsbury, SY4 1JA
Tel: 01939 261616 Fax: 01939 261606
E-mail: info@quillerbooks.com
Website: www.kenilworthpress.co.uk

**Acknowledgements**
Thanks to the following people for their contributions and advice:
Rachael Claridge—Endurance GB Coach
Maggie Pattinson—On the Hoof Distance Training
Steve Beresford—Performance Equestrian
Natasha, Jim and Rebecca Parsler
Barbara Baker
Sally Bell

*Front cover:* Members of the Whaddon Chase Branch of The Pony Club successfully qualifying at Barbury Castle for the Open Endurance Championships in 2011.

# The Pony Club Guide to
# Endurance Riding

by Nicola Parsler

# Contents

# Introduction

The simple motto, *'To complete is to win,'* goes some way to explaining the appeal of endurance riding. It is not a race, but it does require true horsemanship and will challenge, more than any other equestrian discipline, the level of understanding you have for your pony and the depth of your relationship with him. Whilst it is possible to be a highly-skilled rider and yet know little of the animal you are riding, it takes a great deal of skill and understanding to ride him many kilometres in a single day.

When you take part in competitive endurance riding, you are required to cover a given distance at set speeds, guided by maps and markers, and to bring your pony home in the best possible condition. Even at the highest competitive levels, the welfare of the main participant—the pony—is the key consideration.

In Pony Club Endurance riding you can choose to treat the sport as a fun fitness and training exercise—setting your own goals and improving your results each time—or aim to become more competitive, representing your Branch at both Area and National competitions. Any rider and any type of pony can take part by riding within the limits of age, fitness and ability. At the end of an endurance ride placings may be awarded, but it isn't always the fastest who wins. There is nothing quite like the satisfaction of seeing your pony's fitness and recovery rate improving!

# 1. History of Long Distance Riding

## Origins of Long Distance Riding

Modern long distance or 'endurance' riding started in the USA in 1955 when a group of riders set out to prove that modern horsemen had not forgotten how to ride long distances and yet bring horses home unexhausted and fit to go further. They travelled the old Pony Express routes over the Sierra Nevada–100 miles (160km) of rocky trails, from the snow line down to deep canyons along the old Western States Trail, now accepted as the toughest ride in the world. The famous Tevis Cup is still ridden along this route every year. Horses have to carry a total of 73kg (11½ stone) and the first ten horses home carrying that weight are judged for best condition.

In 1966, Tom Quilty launched a 100-mile ride in the Blue Mountains of Sydney, Australia. Steep mountains, quicksands, drops and hills made up this incredibly tough trail. The ride is now held at various similar venues across Australia.

Britain cannot offer the spectacular climbs and descents of these two countries, but the 'Golden Horseshoe', held on Exmoor each year, tests the fitness and endurance of riders who cover 80km (50 miles) across the challenging Exmoor terrain on each of the two days. The primary endurance riding bodies of the UK also host a number of advanced level endurance rides around the country (including international Fédération Équestre Internationale (FEI) events) where riders cover 160km (100 miles) in a day.

## Endurance Riding Today

Although not part of the Olympics, endurance riding is the fastest growing FEI discipline in the world, and the peak of international competitive endurance can be experienced by spectators at both the World Equestrian Games and the World Endurance Championships.

The Pony Club first introduced endurance riding as one of its activities in 1997. The rules were updated in 2009, and further changed in 2013, and endurance riding is now a Pony Club discipline in its own right. There is a National Championship and a range of classes suitable for all Members aged over five years old. Endurance riding is a sport which, at Pony Club level, can be enjoyed by any rider on any type of pony and is a great introduction to many years of pleasure and partnership with your pony.

*Previous page:* The fun of riding out with your Pony Club friends is what makes long distance riding so special.

Aside from The Pony Club there are three main bodies governing endurance riding in the UK today. These are: Endurance GB (EGB) for England and Wales; the Scottish Endurance Riding Club (SERC) for Scotland; and the Irish Long Distance Riding Association (ILDRA) for Northern Ireland. These organisations offer a wide range of endurance ride types and distances, many of which are suitable for novices. All rides are run under strict veterinary control to protect the pony. In less-enlightened days at the end of the last century, huge money was won and lost on distance 'races' and 'trials' where many animals ended up dead. Now, endurance riding focuses heavily on the condition and welfare of the pony, which may be 'spun' (withdrawn) from the ride by the vets at any time.

At a local level there are many bridleway groups, local clubs and associations offering rides, and BHS-affiliated Riding Clubs even have their own national team competition. In 2012 the Riding for the Disabled Association (RDA) formed a partnership with Endurance GB and the FEI to launch Para-Endurance as a recognised discipline for disabled riders. Riders are classified according to their disability and allowed to use additional items of equipment and/or escort riders in order to permit them to participate in both special 'Para' classes and open events. This has made endurance riding into a sport which is truly accessible for all equestrians regardless of age or ability.

Taking a break from Eventing. Mary King and her guide, 14-year-old Abbi Chisholm, completing the Golden Horseshoe together in 2011.

The bronze medal-winning British Young Rider Team at the 2012 European Endurance Championships, Mont le Soie, Belgium.

# Types of Long Distance Ride

Three basic ride-types are commonly offered at endurance riding events.

**NCR (Non-competitive Ride), PR (Social, Training or Pleasure Ride)**
These rides are typically run by local groups/clubs or Pony Club Branches and Centres but many national rides also include one or more PR routes in their schedule. The distance ridden in this type of class is fairly short—usually not more than 32km (20 miles). Generally, you will be asked to present your pony to the vet for a simple trot-up both before and after the ride. Pony Club Level 1 and 2 Training rides are up to 19km (11 miles) and there is no minimum speed; which makes them an ideal starting point for Members wishing to try the sport for the first time. (*See* Chapter 6 for more advice about choosing your first class.)

**Pony Club Competitive Ride, GER (Graded Endurance Ride), Competitive Trail Ride**
These rides may be run by Pony Club Branches or at national events hosted by SERC, ILDRA or EGB. The exact rules vary somewhat between organisations and ride level but all are judged on a combination of speed and the condition of the pony at the finish. The distance ridden

in competitive classes is longer and speeds are generally faster; so the veterinary inspections pre- and post-ride are more stringent (*see* Chapter 7). Although the rides may be called 'competitive', the results are usually judged against set criteria rather than against the performance of other competitors, and all those achieving the required level will be given an award. Pony Club Novice competitive rides (Level 3) start from 20km (12 miles). These rides have to be completed between a set minimum and maximum speed and the pony must pass a vetting with a heart rate of 64bpm (beats per minute) or less within 30 minutes of completion.

**CER (Competitive Endurance Rides), Endurance Ride/Race**
This, the highest level of competition, is restricted to the most experienced pre-qualified ponies and their riders. Events are organised by EGB, SERC, ILDRA and the FEI as part of a National and International competition programme. CERs start from 80km (50 miles) in a day and go up to 160km (100 miles). Ponies all start together and the placings are decided on speed, but the pony must also have passed veterinary inspections at several points along the way in addition to the pre- and post-ride vettings. CERs are very often run alongside lower level classes at the same event and this provides the opportunity for novice competitors to watch some of the best riders in the world compete. It is truly inspiring to watch ponies, with their ears pricked, galloping in for the finish line at the end of such a huge distance!

# 2. What Kind of Pony Do I Need?

The Pony Club Endurance ride levels have been deliberately designed to allow all Members aged five and over to take part. The distances and speeds required, even at Level 5, are well within the scope of most family ponies and horses. Although the sport is commonly perceived as the sole province of Arab horses, this is a misconception and many native types, cobs and hunters have competed successfully at The Pony Club Endurance Championships each year.

A pony who is nimble and sure-footed over difficult terrain is a definite bonus. Longer, flowing paces are also easier on both pony and rider over long distances. The pony who has a lot of up-and-down movement may be wasting energy and can be a wearing ride. You want a pony who goes forward from the leg easily, as having to kick on at every stride will quickly become tiring. However, a pulling, over-excited pony can be an even worse proposition. You must feel comfortable on the pony and that means being happy to ride him over demanding ground where you know you can trust him to be an equal partner, who will not take the upper hand nor leave all the work up to you. You should not have to ride with your heart in your mouth—this sport is supposed to be fun!

The pony must be physically capable to carry out the job without due strain, and an animal that is well put together and of good conformation will do this more easily than one with a straight shoulder and upright pasterns which lack shock absorption.

As they say, '*No foot, no horse,*' so take care of hooves both inside and out by feeding correctly or using additives to promote good hoof growth, and use a hoof preparation to keep the outer horn in good condition. The importance of regular and correct shoeing and trimming goes without saying. A lack of balance will show up as muscle pain and joint damage far more quickly when you are riding for long periods at a time. The attentions of a good farrier will also help you rectify any minor defects in hoof conformation. The Pony Club has two achievement badges which will help you learn about

*Previous page:* Competing for the English team at the Home International in 2009, Natasha Parsler and her 20-year-old Dales pony Shine prove that you don't need an Arab to do endurance.

this aspect of horse and pony care—*Care of the Foot* and *Shoeing*.

Heavier-built ponies will retain their body heat for longer and this means that they will require more active crewing than a finer animal if you are going to reduce their heart rate enough for the final vet. Conversely, a fine-boned, thin-skinned animal may get easily chilled and begin to shiver—which will also result in an elevated pulse. Either type will do well with appropriate crewing; much of the skill in endurance is learning what suits your pony best and making plans accordingly. Above all—whatever size or shape your pony is, he must be sound and have the ability to carry the job through.

Ponies must be at least five years old to compete. Older ponies can take part in endurance rides and compete well at a suitable level, having built up muscle and stamina levels over years of work. Many of the most successful Pony Club Endurance competitors have been veterans in their teens or even twenties. The odd lump and bump may be unsightly but takes nothing off an older pony's performance. He has also seen the world and will take being an endurance pony in his stride, happily enjoying the attentions of your crew.

The mental outlook of a prospective endurance pony should not be underestimated. A calm, laid-back sort of pony will have a low pulse rate, not get over-excited on the ride and will vet at the finish with the minimum of crewing. A more highly-strung animal may struggle with the pressure of other ponies coming up behind or passing, and feel the overwhelming need to be in front of everyone all the time. It is possible for him to be on such a high at the end of the ride that his mental attitude to crewing, the hustle and bustle and pure excitement of all that activity may keep his pulse too high. However, with patience, training and experience most ponies will settle to endurance and such a pony's enthusiastic attitude will be of benefit in keeping him going when things get tough.

It can take a year or two of patiently building up fitness, muscle and experience before you see your best results, whatever age and type of animal you have. If you have a pony that you love, don't give up on him too soon; just remember to ride within the abilities of both your pony and yourself.

# 3. Equipment

Before starting out in endurance riding, many riders ask what type of equipment they will need. The answer, at first, is nothing more than they would use when going out on a long hack. However, the more a rider competes and the longer the distances they have to cover, the sooner they will realise that comfort is a priority for both rider and pony.

# Essential Equipment

Pony Club Endurance rules specify particular items of tack and riding equipment which are not the same as those permitted by EGB, SERC and ILDRA. It is therefore important to check the most recent Rule Book to ensure that you are appropriately kitted out. At rides organised by The Pony Club, including the Championships, there will be a tack check, with the purpose of ensuring that your tack is safe for the job. The stitching on stirrup leathers and reins must be sound; leatherwork must be in good condition; and all tack should fit and be well adjusted. Make sure it is clean and presents a good, workmanlike impression. The Pony Club's *Saddlery* and *Tack Cleaning* achievement badges will help you to learn more about this.

Even if the ride does not have a tack check, well-fitting tack and comfortable clothing is essential for endurance riding. You will be on your pony's back for several hours so any pinching or rubbing will become much more evident than during a half-hour lesson. Looking at the wider field of endurance riding, equipment for pony and rider is designed for safety, comfort and ease of maintenance whilst still allowing a certain amount of individuality. In general terms the tack which you use every day for Pony Club rallies will be adequate provided that it is in good repair and fits well. New tack and/or clothes are not expected, so clean and tidy, comfortable second-hand gear for both pony and rider is completely acceptable.

The equipment described in this chapter will be enough for you to start competing at endurance riding and you will probably already have most of it. As with all equestrian disciplines there is a confusing variety of expensive specialist gear on offer, so it is important to restrict your purchases to those appropriate for your competition level and accepted under Pony Club rules. However, there are some items of special equipment which you will

*Previous page:* When you start endurance riding, it is wise to choose ordinary, well-fitting tack for your pony, and comfortable riding clothes for you.

find helpful as you progress and there are some aspects of endurance riding which you may wish to take into account when choosing what to wear.

## Hats

Your hat must conform to the correct standard: endurance societies and British Riding Clubs have a different one to The Pony Club. Pony Club approved headwear (*see* Rule Book) is acceptable to these societies but *not* the other way round, so you must make sure that you are wearing the right hat. Conventional skull cap type hats can prove to be both heavy and hot when riding longer distances which is why lightweight, ventilated hats (*pictured here*) have become popular among endurance riders. Pony Club Members are permitted to wear these provided that they meet the usual required safety standards. These hats are only acceptable at endurance rides however—not at other Pony Club rallies or events—so unless you are doing a lot of longer rides it is probably more sensible to use your normal hat.

## Footwear

Most endurance riders favour short riding boots and half chaps instead of tall boots because tall boots tend to be too hot for the time spent riding. This is another area where you need to be careful as Pony Club rules are not the same as those for other endurance societies. (*See* Rule Book for details.) Your usual jodhpur boots with a smooth sole will be acceptable to all organisations but if you are going to be running across slippery terrain leading your pony for parts of the route, or mounting and dismounting frequently for gates, then you may find that they offer limited grip. In these cases trainer-style riding boots offer an alternative and Pony Club Endurance rules do allow for this provided that you ride in a caged stirrup.

A wide range of half chaps are available. The most important thing is that they fit well and are comfortable but when buying a new pair you should give consideration to features such as ease of cleaning, breathable fabric (*pictured above-right*) or reflective strips. Unlike other Pony Club disciplines, coloured chaps and reflective stripes are permitted for safety reasons as they can help improve visibility. (However, decorative tassels and fringes are not allowed.)

As with all things, if you do purchase specialist footwear/chaps for endurance riding you should be aware that it may not be acceptable to use them for other Pony Club events.

## Map Case

You will need a map case (a clear, waterproof plastic case on a strap, similar to the one *pictured here*) to hold ride instructions and your map. As map cases tend to flap you must make sure that the cord is long enough to fit over your shoulder and hold the case snugly under your arm.

### HINT

Putting your number bib on over the top of the map case strap also helps to reduce flapping and twisting. A shirt with a collar is recommended because the strap of the map case can rub your neck and become uncomfortable. It is a good idea to put your map into the case upside down so that when you look at it whilst riding, it will be the right way up!

## Water

It is important to carry a drink because it is surprisingly easy to become dehydrated during an endurance ride as you lose body fluids by sweating and are not able to replace them quickly enough. Almost all endurance riders use some form of saddle-mounted water bottle and holder. A plastic drink container with a top you pull up with your teeth is the best type. If you do not have a bottle carrier (right) then take a high energy sports drink with you—the sort that comes in squashy packs that you can

slip into a pocket. Keeping hydrated on rides is crucial. Most riders would seek out water for their pony on long rides but, in the excitement of competition, might forget to drink themselves.

Dehydration can cause serious problems—from headaches to dizziness—and at worst can make you become confused, unable to make decisions, and make you feel dreadful. Reminding their rider to have a drink at crew points is an important duty for the crew.

Water is also vital for the pony. If the day is hot or your pony is not fit enough he may lose so much fluid that he becomes dehydrated, and when it comes to the final vetting he will not pass. Always make sure that you allow the pony to drink as much as he wants whenever you have access to water. If you have to cross a stream, for example, pause for a moment to see if he would like a drink. Ride maps will often indicate where there is water available en route. (*See* Chapter 7 on *Crewing* for more information on pony and rider care during the ride.)

## First Aid Kit

It is wise, and in some cases obligatory, to take a first aid kit. The Pony Club recommends that it contains the following:

- Triangular bandage.
- Wound dressing.
- Vet wrap (or similar).
- Space blanket (foil ones fold into a tiny package).
- Glucose sweets or mint cake.
- Whistle.
- A small length of string. (Baler twine will do, but leather shoelaces are unbeatable.)
- Some riders like to include a folding hoof pick.
- If you require any medication such as an asthma inhaler it is also sensible to carry this with you.
- You may also wish to carry a snack for the rider such as a cereal bar.

The entire kit can be carried in a bum bag or saddle pannier. The Pony Club recommends that it is carried on the rider's person because if they have a fall and their first aid kit is attached to the saddle it may be unavailable just when it is needed most. At the very least a rider should carry a wound dressing in a pocket. However, if you opt for a saddle pannier you need to ensure that it is firmly fastened so that it does not bounce up and down on your pony's back.

Pony riding can be a dangerous sport so you are strongly recommended to undertake some basic first aid training whatever discipline you choose to participate in. In addition, endurance riders are often riding for long periods out of sight of stewards or other immediate sources of assistance. The Pony Club runs two achievement badges which will help you prepare for any accidents—*Human First Aid* and *Equine First Aid*.

## Mobile Phone

Carrying a mobile phone with you (in case you need to contact your crew or the emergency services) is a sensible precaution. You can buy special cases for them which fit onto your arm, or else the phone can be slipped inside a bum bag. However you should be aware that some rides will take you into areas where there is a poor mobile signal. This is why your first aid kit should always contain a whistle for summoning help.

## Medical Card

Pony Club rules state that all Members *must* wear a medical armband on their arm whilst competing in endurance.

(N.B. It is not considered safe to wear it on the leg as this may make it difficult to access in the event of an accident) The medical card should contain details of any pre-existing medical conditions and medication, emergency contact details and doctor's contact information. Some rides will also require you to lodge these details with the Ride Secretary so it is important to check the rules. Carrying emergency contact and medical information on you is a sensible precaution even if you are not riding under rules.

## Whips and Spurs

If you carry a stick on the ride it must be under 75cm long (30in). Whips may not be used during the veterinary presentation to assist the trot up or on the final loop of a competitive endurance ride (CER). Spurs are not permitted under any circumstances.

# Clothing for the Rider

In endurance you are riding for a long time. Comfortable clothes that give you freedom of movement to ride, mount and dismount easily and which are also suitable for the weather conditions are important.

If you go to a ride run by one of the affiliated bodies you will notice that many endurance riders ride in a particular colour scheme. Often bright colours are chosen to allow their crews (helpers) to easily identify them within a group of riders and increase visibility on the roads. Being bright does not mean that the rider should not look neat and tidy so once a particular colour scheme is chosen, hat, tack and clothing is usually coordinated. There are no rules within Pony Club Endurance limiting the choice of colours for either tack or rider's clothing but your Pony Club Branch will probably have their own team/Branch colours for competitions.

## Outer Wear

Outer clothing will depend on several factors. Usually weather plays a major part in the decision process, and as this can change constantly it is often better to have several layers of clothing that can be easily removed or added to depending on conditions. Layers could include lightweight fleeces, gilets, lightweight showerproof jackets or heavy-duty waterproof riding jackets, depending upon the weather and the terrain being ridden across. (N.B. It is not advisable to ride in hooded jackets or jumpers as the flapping hood could easily become caught.) British weather is notorious for its unpredictability. Dress sensibly and plan ahead for possible changes.

Cold, wet, miserable weather can have its problems. A lightweight waterproof tied to the back of your saddle may save you from getting thoroughly chilled and suffering from hypothermia (being so cold that you can't function properly).

It is surprisingly easy to become overheated and dehydrated even during a novice-level

A tidy but comfortable and practical turn out is best for endurance.

25

endurance ride in cool weather, so it is important that your base layer should be breathable and not too heavy. However, long sleeves—at least ones which cover your shoulders—are recommended, as a sleeveless top may leave you unbearably burnt by the sun and wind. A collar is also advised to prevent rubbing, as riders will need to carry a map which is usually fastened over the shoulders in a map case. Polo shirts are a popular choice but specific sports base layers can also be used.

## Body Protectors

The use of body protectors is a matter of personal choice. The majority of endurance riders do not use them because, as previously mentioned, it is relatively easy to become dehydrated and this will have a negative effect on your riding ability and judgement. Pony Club rules do not require you to wear a body protector because there are no jumps involved. However, if you do choose to ride in one, make sure that it fits well and is comfortable and ensure that you carry fluids with you so that you can take regular drinks during the ride.

## Legwear

Well-fitting, comfortable jodhpurs are the most commonly used legwear and should be more than sufficient at Pony Club level. You may however wish to give some thought to the material they are made from as high levels of nylon or polyester in the fabric can make them become hot and cause rubs over longer distances. Heavyweight fabrics (such as in denim-style jodhpurs) can also cause problems because they take longer to dry out if it rains and clinging, damp fabric is extremely uncomfortable.

As you progress you will probably see specialist riding tights being worn by some advanced competitors. Traditional jodhpurs have an inner seam, which together with their cotton/polyester fabric can cause friction burns and pinching when used during very long endurance rides. To solve this problem, American trail riders came up with riding

---

**HINT**

With regards to colour, there are no rules within Pony Club Endurance, but you will probably get quite grubby during a ride so it is perhaps advisable not to wear your best cream breeches!

tights or leggings. The tights are manufactured from a lightweight, breathable, wicking, four-way-stretch material that is designed to move with the body—thus eliminating the chance of rubs and pinches. There is no inner seam on them, they dry quickly, and you can get them in a variety of fabric weights. Some are even available with seat and knee padding to protect sensitive areas.

## Underwear

Underwear may not be the first thing you think about, but after several miles of hard riding you may wish that you had given more attention to it. Cotton with Lycra (for stretch) is better than Nylon. For male riders especially, close fitting underwear is preferable to loose cotton boxers which can become rucked up and cause soreness from rubbing. Female riders will also want to give consideration to a supportive bra.

## Gloves

Gloves are recommended for endurance riding. They protect your fingers from chafing on the reins and improve your grip, especially in wet conditions.

# Gear for the Pony

Leather tack is a quality item and should be treated as such. It looks smart and with good cleaning and maintenance it will last many years. However, many endurance riders now favour tack manufactured from synthetic materials such as polypropylene webbing or BioThane, a strong coated webbing material. Synthetic tack is practical in that it stands a lot of abuse in foul weather and is very tolerant of the amount of water that your crew is likely to get over it. It will rinse out and dry with no harm, whereas leather tack will stiffen and will need loving attention to keep it in good condition.

## Bridles

When you first start endurance riding the best advice is to simply use the bridle that you already have and that your pony is used to. However a synthetic bridle can be a sensible investment if you are competing regularly and wish to protect your leather tack.

Synthetic combination bridles (*pictured overleaf*) are used extensively in endurance riding. These bridles convert to head collars and halters by allowing the bit to be removed, which is useful when you need your pony to drink and eat whilst out riding. Reins are clipped on rather than buckled so that you can easily unclip one side, leaving a long line for leading. Breastplates and martingales which have a clip attaching to a 'D' in the centre of the girth make it easy to remove them without having to undo the girth.

A BioThane bridle.

Synthetic bridles are available in a wide range of colours which can be coordinated with clothing for rider/pony identification. Be aware, though, that, whilst Pony Club Endurance does not place any restriction on colours, this is not the case with other disciplines where synthetic tack is only permitted in the traditional colours of black and brown.

The choice of materials is down to personal preference and budget. Webbing is a lighter-weight material and tends to be cheaper. However webbing needs to have sweat washed out of it, whilst BioThane (or a similar material with a shiny surface) will just wipe clean. BioThane is also more durable but it is generally more expensive and much heavier. Neoprene or sheepskin protection can be used on sensitive-skinned animals over the headpiece and noseband.

## Reins

It is worth considering the style of rein you use as they can become slippery when wet. Reins with periodic stops or rubber grips are best. It is also possible to get reins in a variety of styles in synthetic materials which are designed to be less prone to slipping. However, beware of very rough or thick reins as these can cause chafing of your fingers.

## Saddle

A well-fitting saddle is essential. Correct fit and comfort of the saddle have a direct bearing on your pony's ability to complete the ride in first-rate condition. Never underestimate the damage a poorly-fitting saddle can do. Bear in mind though, due to the length of time your pony will be carrying both you and a saddle, coupled with his change in shape as he becomes fitter, the fit does need to be checked at regular intervals.

Synthetic saddles can be a practical choice because they are lightweight, adjustable and suffer less in wet conditions. There are also some new concepts in saddle design and fitting which have been aimed specifically at endurance riders. These new designs aim to enable the pony to travel further distances, and to carry the weight of the rider with less stress than before and to perform to the very best of his ability by freeing the shoulder. Specialist saddles like these are unlikely to be necessary at Pony Club level but they are acceptable within the rules. However, if the saddle has fixed stirrup points then you must ride in a caged or safety stirrup and styles which do not have the required 5cm (2in) clearance over the withers (such as some treeless saddles) would not be allowed.

## Seat Savers

These are a useful addition for riders wishing to ride longer distances. Not only do they protect the saddle but also other parts of the anatomy! Ones made from natural materials such as sheepskin or with memory foam padding tend to be the most popular.

## Girths

It is relatively easy for wet or muddy girths to cause rubs during an endurance ride. Girth sleeves or girths made with Neoprene are easier to clean during crewing and less likely to cause friction against the pony.

## Saddlecloths and Numnahs

Numnahs and saddlecloths made from materials with shock-absorbing properties (such as polypads or sheepskin), or which are designed to improve airflow, are popular for obvious reasons. However, as with the rest of the tack, the main thing is to ensure a comfortable fit. Rubs can occur if the numnah is rucked up, pressing on the withers or dirty. Ensure that the numnah is pulled right up into the pommel and cantle of the saddle and lies flat under the flaps in order to prevent rubbing. As with girths, if your ride has a midway vet hold then it is a good idea to have a clean spare to put on for the second half of the ride.

**HINT**

When entering a ride which has a compulsory vet hold it is wise to carry a spare girth and numnah so you can change it at the midway point.

## Stirrups

As riders increase the distance they ride, more stress and pressure is put on legs, feet and joints. Traditional metal stirrups, whilst ideal for everyday riding, are inflexible and heavy. Endurance stirrups, on the other hand, are made from high-impact plastic to be extremely lightweight, and they are also designed to provide a wider base for the foot to reduce fatigue and offer cushioning from the soft tread for joints and muscles. These stirrups are, however, quite large and younger Members may need to use them in conjunction with a caged front because a small foot could slip through.

## Boots and Bandages

You may not present your pony to the vetting in boots or bandages, but if you are using them they must be on for the tack check if there is one. Don't use them unless you really need them, because there is a risk of small particles of grit or debris getting trapped under them, and this can cause rubbing during a long-distance ride.

## Hoof Boots and Shoes

If your pony is normally shod then it is a good idea to plan your farrier's visits so that he has fairly new shoes on the day of competition. No more than two weeks in advance of the competition is ideal. Nothing is more guaranteed to spoil a good ride than a lost shoe. Many rides will have a farrier in attendance who can come out to you on course if needed and so having a spare set of shoes amongst your crewing kit is a sensible precaution. A lot of distance riders also routinely carry some sort of 'spare hoof' in the form of a boot for the pony as fitting this can be a lot less time consuming than calling for the farrier.

There are a wide variety of hoof boots available, including those intended to be worn instead of shoes. These are increasing in

Hoof boots can offer useful additional protection for the barefoot pony.

popularity and offer a normally barefoot pony some protection against hard and stony going. Although, due to the wear and stresses placed on the hoof over long distances, the majority of endurance ponies are shod, properly fitted hoof boots can be used successfully as an alternative. If you are using hoof boots to ride in as an alternative to shoes, then you may choose whether to leave them on or remove them for the vetting.

At the lower levels a pony with good feet that is used to going barefoot will be able to compete quite happily without additional protection. However, you will need to plan your ride carefully to avoid too much fast work over stony ground and make use of verges and softer areas as much as possible.

## Plaiting

If you have a pony with a long mane it is a good idea to tidy it up with several long plaits. This helps to keep the neck cool, makes it easier for you to get water down his neck when crewing, and keeps it out of the way of the reins. If the going is likely to be very muddy and wet and your pony has a long tail you could tape and tie it up out of the way, so that it does not get continually tangled in his legs. Plaiting the mane and tail as if for the show ring is unnecessary.

## Tail Ribbons

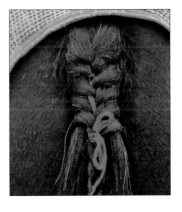

If your pony might kick then it is considered good practice to put a red ribbon in its tail. A young or novice pony wears green and a stallion blue. As the ribbon needs to stay in for a long time it is important to ensure that it is securely fastened.

If you see a pony wearing any of these ribbons on their tail whilst on the ride then it is advisable to approach/pass with caution.

## Sponge

The other useful item is a simple sponge on a string attached to the saddle. In hot conditions it enables you to make use of any available natural water (streams etc..) to sponge your pony while he is drinking. Keeping the pony's temperature down will help maintain condition throughout the ride and make it easier for your crew to cool him at checkpoints and at the finish.

# Technology

## Online Mapping

If you are going to a ride in an unfamiliar part of the country then it can help you to plan your ride if you look up the route on one of the online mapping services that offer satellite photographic views. By comparing these pictures with your ride map you can get a good idea of the type of going and landmarks to navigate by.

## GPS

GPS monitors are permitted under Pony Club rules and can be a very useful aid for training and competition if you are competing regularly. There are a wide range of models on the market but the simplest will keep track of the distance you have travelled and show you your average speed. This makes for an 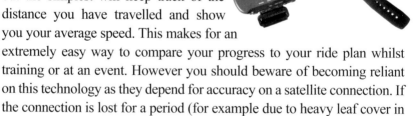 extremely easy way to compare your progress to your ride plan whilst training or at an event. However you should beware of becoming reliant on this technology as they depend for accuracy on a satellite connection. If the connection is lost for a period (for example due to heavy leaf cover in woodland) then the information given will be incorrect.

## Heart Rate Monitors

These are mainly used by keen, competitive riders competing at high-mileage events where they want to continually monitor the heart rate. A heart rate monitor (illustrated opposite) typically consists of one transmitter slipped under the girth, near where you would use a

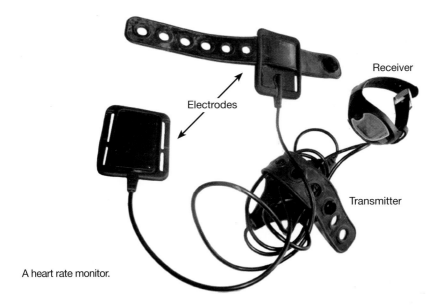

Receiver

Electrodes

Transmitter

A heart rate monitor.

stethoscope, and another under the saddle panels. The receiver can be worn on your wrist or the saddle and gives a digital read-out. It can be a great training aid as well as enabling you to learn how your pony performs under various conditions. Some types combine the functions of a GPS with those of the heart rate monitor.

Veterinary-style heart rate monitors are also a great crewing aid. These have the sensor mounted on a handle which enables the monitor to be held against the pony's girth area. The monitor offers a very quick and easy way to assess the pony's heart/recovery rate at the end of the ride. However, you need to be aware that monitors work by taking an average reading so are not as accurate as a stethoscope. All types of heart rate monitor require a proper contact in order to work accurately. This can be provided by coating the sensors with water-based gel although it is not usually necessary once the pony's coat is wet.

**HINT**

As mentioned at the start of this chapter, most of the specialised products discussed here are not necessary to start endurance riding, but will help both rider and pony as they progress through the sport. You should also remember that the day of the ride is not the time to try out new equipment!

# 4. Preparation and Fitness

Endurance riding is about fitness. You and your pony must be fit for the job. Endurance is not about racing or getting there faster than the next person: it is all about skill, knowing your pony, and using this knowledge to present him at the final vetting with a low pulse, an unbruised mouth and a flowing, sound in-hand trot-up for the vet, with both of you feeling that you could go on for a few more miles. This section will discuss rider and pony fitness, and how to work towards your ride and complete it successfully.

# Rider Fitness

How many times have you heard it said that riders just sit on top and enjoy themselves while the ponies do all the work? And how many times have you been really tired after a long ride or a hard lesson? Tiredness makes you feel heavier and also makes you less able to maintain a good balance. Eventually you lose concentration and ride on 'auto-pilot'—and that is when things can go wrong.

You don't need to be super-fit but you *do* need to be able to ride in balance with your pony for the whole duration of the ride. Obviously, the longer the ride the fitter you need to be. As a guide, for a Level 3 Pony Club ride you would expect to be in the saddle for two to three hours.

You should also ideally be fit enough to get off and jog along with your pony—stretching your legs and easing his back over long distances, or to help him if he's lost a shoe. The ground is easier for your pony to cope with if you are off his back, letting him balance himself and pick his way. Take the reins over his head and give him enough length to stretch. Too tight and he won't be able to balance himself and will rely on you to hold him up—probably walking on your toes—and you will be more of a hindrance than a help to him. It is possible to go faster over rough ground jogging beside your pony than sitting on his back. All this means that you have to be fit enough to neither get out of breath, get a 'stitch' in your side, nor have legs that feel like lead!

Fitness on a ride also involves taking care of your energy levels. Tiredness can be caused by not having an adequate meal. Don't skip breakfast because you are too excited to eat: you will need plenty of high-

*Previous page:* Knowing that your pony is fit enough for the miles ahead will give you and your teammates confidence when you compete.

energy fuel later in the day. Take something in your pocket or bag—but not something which will melt or get squashed. Dried fruit, marzipan or a muesli-type bar are good. Drink plenty of fluids to avoid getting thirsty and to prevent the possibility of dehydration. Isotonic drinks (but not the fizzy sort!) are good for longer rides and will help to replenish your salt and water levels. If you have a crew (*see* Chapter 8) make sure that they have drinks and snacks for you to replenish your supplies.

## Riding Effectively

You need to be able to ride as lightly and well balanced as possible, going forwards easily at the trot and not rising too high out of the saddle (which wastes energy). Have your stirrups at a comfortable length. You need to be able to mount lightly—so as not to jolt your pony's back muscles—and not to have to mountaineer up into the saddle. Check your stirrup length: you won't have to jump anything on the ride and short stirrups can cause a lot of stress and fatigue on ankle, knee and hip joints. It has been said that pain is a great teacher: once both you and your pony are going comfortably together it means that you are riding well.

As well as physical fitness you have to have the right mental attitude to want to ride for a long distance. If you get bored after an hour's hack and you don't like being wet, cold, hot, tired or thirsty, perhaps you are looking at the wrong sport. Endurance includes all of these—and more! It is about getting to know your pony; knowing how he feels about his partnership with you and how you feel about yours with him. You need to know when he should ease up for his own good, yet at the same time know how far you can push him under the pressure of competition. Endurance riding will improve your horsemanship, your understanding of your pony and your riding ability as you combine all three to compete safely and successfully. It is a great adventure of discovery about yourself, your pony and the country around you. Good schooling and good horsemanship can save precious seconds, and your pony's health.

It is also important to pay attention to your pony's paces. The ideal gait varies between ponies, and your pony may do better in either trot or canter. When training, check your pony's heart rate and speed of recovery after a good stretch of trot or canter to see which pace is less tiring for him. A good trot should be flowing, steady, and not too up-and-down or bouncy. A good canter is also steady, and the power should be coming from your pony's hind quarters. They should not be leaning on the forehand. Canter is especially useful for going up hills, so pay attention to the terrain. By leaning forward up steep hills you can free the pony's quarters and help him move forwards more easily—even if you have to hold on to a piece of mane while you do so. If you are riding downhill, ease your weight back a little and give your pony enough rein to allow him to see where he is going. Your pony should be able to keep the same pace for a long distance, so it is your responsibility not to push him too fast. Your aim should be for a consistent, steady pace as constant changes will be tiring for both of you.

## Knowing Your Pony

The whole sport of endurance riding is based on a good working relationship between rider and horse. You have to know his capabilities. You need to know what is normal for him so that you can tell if he becomes stressed, as well as how far and how fast he can go. You will become a better horseman the longer you spend in his company and on his back. He must have confidence in you as well as you having confidence in him. Together you will have a lot of fun and find out more of the meaning of true horsemanship.

# Pony Fitness

Whatever the discipline you are intending to compete in it is important that your pony is fit for the job. Endurance riding is often mistaken for a quiet hack but in fact it is probably one of the most demanding of all equestrian disciplines. Within The Pony Club parameters most ponies will be able to cope, however it is important to look at your future goals and work towards them from the start. You should include them in your training plan.

If you ride your pony often and he is fit and active throughout the year, it is likely that low-level endurance riding will not put too much strain on him. If you only ride occasionally and your pony is not fit, you should carefully weigh up how much you can expect from him. It is not safe, sensible or kind to make an overweight, un-toned animal compete in a sport for which he is not prepared. Many ponies suffer from a combination of obesity and over-enthusiasm—unable to know when they have had enough. They could, literally, go on until they drop.

If you intend to compete, you should plan an exercise and feeding

With careful management and training, 26-year-old Barnabas is still fit enough to enjoy rides up to 40km.

schedule in advance. Getting really fit can't be done in odd days here and there. Legs need to be hardened by steady, slow work built up over a period of time, and the lungs and heart must be strengthened the same way so that they can stand the stress put on them under competition. Unfit muscles lead to a greater likelihood of damage, and this applies to the rider as well as to the pony—so aim to get fit together. Plenty of active walking to toughen bones and tendons, steady trotting up hills and a little cantering to activate lungs and heart (for the pony) and jogging alongside (for you) should be of benefit to both of you.

A sensible programme for getting your pony fit can be found in the *Manual of Horsemanship*. However, whilst the basic principles are the same for every pony, common sense must always prevail as the amount of time you need to spend on each stage will vary somewhat between ponies. The naturally-athletic type finds it easier to attain a good fitness level with little effort, while the heavier native breeds, or those already overweight and less forward-going, can present a real challenge. Younger animals in particular will often take longer to build base level fitness than an older animal with years of work behind him. It is up to the rider to devise a fittening programme based on personal knowledge of the particular pony or to seek advice from a riding instructor who knows the animal. The Pony Club's *Fitness* achievement badge will help you learn how to do this.

Base work (which helps to build and strengthen muscles, tendons and bones) is the most important part of any fitness programme, and is something to build upon year after year. Cardiovascular fitness, involving the heart and lungs, is relatively easy for ponies, who are natural athletes, but without base fitness nothing holds together!

The important first stage of walk work should last a good three to six weeks, depending on your pony's existing level of fitness. You can add some trot into the programme after week three unless your pony is recovering from a strain or a long period of rest—in which case build up the level of work more gradually. Even if you have continued to work throughout the year it is a good habit to get into this type of programme: it gives you the chance to really see and feel how your pony is going! By weeks five and six you should be able to walk and trot for up to two hours with ease!

After six weeks or so your pony should be fit enough to do some canter work in the open. This will further build his muscle and help to clear his wind. It is good practice, once a week, to measure your pony's heart rate with a stethoscope (more about this later in the book) after you have had a brisk canter for about 400m (a quarter of a mile). The quicker his heart rate returns to its natural resting level the fitter he is becoming. The usual resting heart rate will be between 35 and 45bpm, but you need to know what your pony's normal at-rest heart rate is in order to correctly judge his fitness. Keeping a training log is a sensible way to check on progress.

Girth and back areas need to be tough enough to withstand having the saddle (and you) on them for a long time. Applying surgical spirit is the traditional way of toughening up the soft areas, but gradually building up the fitness and condition of the pony is utterly essential.

## HINT

Most of us probably just tick over through the winter and during term time—a little bit of work here and there, and then a build-up for a few weeks before an event or camp. That build-up cannot be made to happen the week before—which should be time for a little restful work—because if you're not fit enough, working for just one week won't make you fit! Go for a restful hack or light schooling session in the week before an event, to avoid tiring your pony.

Don't forget that a fit pony needs a fit rider—you need to work on yourself too, why not try running with your pony now and again—enjoy each others company and have lots of fun.

There are no short cuts to getting you both fit, but once you attain a reasonable level of fitness it takes very little effort to sustain it as long as you know the physical capabilities of both you and your pony.

# Understanding Speed and Distance

Speed and distance are fundamental elements of endurance. Without understanding how far and how fast you've gone, it is impossible to pace yourselves. As you gain experience you will learn how fast your pony's walk, trot and steady canter are in kilometres per hour (km/h). Some ponies put a lot of energy into their paces but spend most of that effort going up and down rather than forwards: such a pony may feel like he is covering ground more quickly than is really happening purely due to the amount of energy he is using up.

The first part of your training should include finding a route you ride regularly and getting someone to help you measure its distance on a map. (*See* Chapter 6.) You can assess how far you've ridden by using landmarks along the way, and by timing it too you can work out how fast you walk, trot and canter. The circuit doesn't have to be far: 4 or 5km (2½–3 miles) is fine, and it can then become an important part of your training plan.

The formula for working out your speed is SPEED = DISTANCE ÷ TIME. Take a watch with you on your rides to work out the time they take. (*See* Chapter 6 on *Planning and Paperwork.*)

Overall it's worth remembering if you are hacking out, schooling and attending lessons and rallies, you will be fine to compete at Pony Club level endurance—however getting an understanding of different levels of fitness will help to prepare you for the future. Understanding how fast you go, staying in a rhythm in order to conserve energy etc. will really help you in all disciplines.

Training too much is as bad as not training enough—so don't expect your pony to stay at peak fitness all the time. That is bad and harmful in practice—and remember that if you keep them too fit they'll only get naughty—train for the job you want them to do and remember the importance of chilling-out time!

# 5. Feeding for Endurance

The key to successful competition is achieving a balance between health and performance. Stress caused by the rigours of training and competing can affect a horse's digestive health and result in problems like colic or gastric ulcers. A competition horse's diet should therefore be as sympathetic to the digestive system as possible. The rules of feeding are based on many years of knowledge, and implementing them as thoroughly as you can is the first step to keeping your horse healthy enough to train and compete.

# Fuelling Endurance Work

Endurance riding involves work for relatively long periods of time at speeds lower than those required by disciplines such as polo or racing. The horse therefore works most of the time *aerobically* (energy is produced using oxygen) which allows the waste products from the energy production to be cleared from cells quickly enough for the process to keep on going. When horses work at high speeds, energy is produced *anaerobically* (without oxygen) but the body can only sustain it for a limited time until fatigue occurs. Endurance exercise is largely aerobic, but there may nonetheless still be times when the horse works anaerobically—such as climbing a very steep hill. (*See* The Pony Club publication, *Stablemates: Fit for the Bit.*)

Just like humans, horses utilise energy from sources such as oils, fats, carbohydrates and protein, but they can also derive energy from fibre due to a population of microbes that live in their digestive system. Fibre, along with fats and oils, cannot be broken down anaerobically, but just by aerobic metabolism, and it is therefore a very useful energy source for the endurance horse. It is *slow release*, which means it is particularly useful for horses and ponies that tend to be over-excitable or fizzy.

Carbohydrates (like starch and sugar) can be broken down aerobically *or* anaerobically and are known as *quick-release* energy sources. They are present in higher levels in feed materials such as cereals and molasses but foods thought of as 'high in fibre' may also contain sugar and starch. Grass, for example, is probably the greatest source of sugar for most horses that are turned out—and grass hay is typically 10% sugar. Thus, even relatively high-fibre diets will still be supplying some sugar that can be used to fuel anaerobic metabolism.

*Previous page:* Ensuring the horse remains hydrated is an important consideration.

# Slow-Release Energy Sources

Slow-release energy sources (such as fibre, fats and oils) are especially useful for endurance horses and ponies.

## Fibre

Fibre is broken down by the microorganisms that live in the horse's digestive system by a process known as 'fermentation'. Fibre molecules are joined together by complex bonds and it takes the microorganisms a long time to break them down—up to three days for very indigestible fibres—which is why fibre is said to be a slow-release energy source.

Different types of fibre range in digestibility (the ease with which they can be broken down by the microorganisms). *Less digestible* fibres (such as straw) take longer to break down and so may pass through the gut before all the energy they contain can be released. This isn't always a bad thing as good doers and overweight individuals require plenty of fibre (to maintain a healthy digestive system) with as little energy as possible (so they don't put on more weight).

At the other end of the digestibility scale, sugar beet contains *very digestible* fibre that is readily broken down by the microbes in the gut

Hay is a good source of digestible fibre.

and so provides lots of energy. Contrary to what its name suggests, it is actually very low in sugar—especially if molasses haven't been added—because much of the sugar content is extracted for use in the human food industry. By the time the beet is given as animal food, all that is left is a fibrous residue, which is a great feed for horses—particularly endurance ones—as it contains less than 5% sugar. An additional benefit (especially to endurance horses) is that sugar beet is fed soaked to horses and so takes water into the digestive system, which helps to keep the horse hydrated.

Horses are herbivores, and as a result fibre is very important for maintaining gut health and should therefore be the basis of all a horse's rations—even a horse competing at the very highest levels. Insufficient fibre in the diet can result in gastric ulcers, colic, weight loss and loose droppings, so it is vital that plenty is fed.

## Fats and Oils

Fats and oils are another source of slow-release energy and contain roughly two-and-a-quarter times more energy than carbohydrates. This makes them a useful way of supplying lots of energy in a relatively small volume of feed. Endurance horses competing over long distances are often fed quite high levels of oil because they need a lot of energy. Whilst some oil is likely to be beneficial for horses and ponies competing in Pony Club Endurance competitions, it must not be overfed as many ponies won't need the high level of energy it provides and might therefore put on too much weight. Poor doers or those competing over longer distances can benefit from more oil in the ration.

The quality of oils varies, and better ones contain more of the essential fatty acids omega-3 and omega-6. The best oils for omega-3 are fish, linseed or hemp oil which are used in relatively small amounts to meet omega-3 requirements (which are lower than omega-6). Soya, rape seed and vegetable oil are more commonly used in larger quantities to supply higher levels of energy. No matter which oil you choose to use, it is important to ensure that it is of high quality and approved for human or animal consumption.

Many commercially-prepared feeds contain oil and when larger quantities are included it is typically balanced with additional vitamin E. If you are using straights you can add oil separately but do ensure that sufficient vitamin E is added by feeding a good-quality supplement or balancer.

# Keeping Your Endurance Horse Healthy

The basic rules of feeding are designed to promote a healthy digestive system. Trying to feed your horse as naturally as possible is also a good way of reducing the risk of digestive upsets occurring. For example, using fibre and oil as energy sources and only using cereals if they are really required significantly reduces the risk of diseases such as laminitis and colic. A high-fibre diet also helps to retain fluid in the hind gut for longer, helping to maintain hydration.

## The Importance of a Balanced Diet

Although needed in much smaller amounts than other nutrients, vitamins and minerals are very important for health and performance. Minerals perform a variety of roles in the body: calcium, for example, is a component of bones and teeth, and electrolytes facilitate the transfer of nerve impulses. Vitamins are important because they are components of antioxidants, the body's defence against free radicals (produced as a normal part of metabolism) that increase in number as a result of exercise.

B vitamins are produced naturally as a by-product of fibre being digested by bacteria in the gut. One of the most well-known B vitamins is biotin, found in hoof horn tissue. Other B vitamins are involved in the metabolism of energy, which is why they are often added to manufactured feeds and supplements intended for horses competing or in harder work. It is also worth considering that the less fibre that is fed, the lower the amount of internally-produced B vitamins there will be, which is another reason why competition horses may benefit from feeds or supplements that contain B vitamins (as unfortunately, they are often fed less fibre).

Good doers or overweight horses may not require the level of energy that a competition feed provides, so in these situations it is perfectly acceptable to use a lower-energy feed and top up with a balancer or supplement to ensure that the correct levels of essential nutrients are supplied. This would apply when using straights too as they should be balanced with a supplement or balancer designed for the level of work the horse is doing.

## Electrolytes

Electrolytes are minerals that dissolve once in the body and gain a positive or negative charge. They are involved in neuromuscular function and also affect hydration. They are soluble in water and are consequently lost from the body in sweat and urine. For competition horses, the losses in sweat can be considerable, and hot and humid conditions significantly increase the amount of electrolytes lost. The need to supplement electrolytes for horses and ponies competing in very short rides may be much less. However, those that sweat-up through over-excitement and horses and ponies that have previously had muscle problems such as ERS (also known as 'tying-up' or 'azoturia'), are likely to benefit from supplementation with electrolytes.

Electrolytes are salts, so if they were included in feed at sufficient levels to replace those lost when working, the feed would taste very salty and would probably be unpalatable to most horses. For this reason electrolytes tend to be supplied as supplements that can be added to the feed or water. They can also be in the form of a paste that is administered via an oral syringe (*pictured below*), just like a wormer.

If adding electrolytes to water, it is recommended that plain water is made available as well since some horses might not drink the water with the electrolytes added, and unless there is an alternative offered the danger is that they won't drink at all and will become dehydrated.

If adding electrolytes to feed, the feed should be dampened to promote good absorption of the electrolytes. It is important to note that if a horse is already significantly dehydrated and electrolytes are supplied without additional fluids, they can make the dehydration worse.

Significant losses of electrolytes result in fatigue and poor performance. As they are water-soluble they can't be stored in the body which means that horses in regular hard work may require electrolytes daily. But it is also possible to use electrolytes around a specific period of harder work. For example, supplementing the day before a competition should mean the horse starts with full reserves of electrolytes. They can then be used on the day of the competition and the day after to replace what has been used.

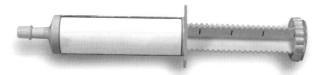

## Promoting Gut Health with Digestive Aids

The microorganisms in the gut are important to the horse for breaking down fibre but also have a role in the horse's defence against harmful bacteria. The good bugs in the gut are affected adversely if too much starch is present, creating a very acidic environment: as they die off, the chain of events leading to laminitis can begin and, in the absence of good bacteria, harmful bacteria become established. Other factors are also able to disrupt the population of good bacteria in the gut: excitement or nervousness can speed up the movement of the gut (which is known as 'peristalsis') so that food moves through it more quickly, and the part-digested food can carry good bacteria out with it. This will have happened, for example, if a horse has got loose droppings when he has travelled and competed.

Various types of digestive aids can also be used to promote gut health. Live yeast is relatively well-researched for horses and is an approved additive under EU regulations. Yeast cells are found in the horse's gut and are part of the fibre digestion process because they help to break open the fibre molecules. Live yeast is often described as 'yeast culture': the culture is simply the material that the yeast cells have been grown on and often includes metabolites such as amino acids and B vitamins. Live yeast is often referred to as a probiotic, but it is important to note that this term is also used to describe live bacteria. Currently there are no live bacteria approved for use in horses in Europe and so probiotics for horses should only contain live yeast.

Prebiotics—another type of digestive aid—are feed materials that the horse can't break down itself but are specific to friendly bacteria in the gut that only they can digest. Prebiotics are used to boost the numbers of friendly bacteria by feeding them well so that they reproduce in greater numbers. There is some evidence to show that prebiotics can also be beneficial in the stomach for helping to reduce the risk of gastric ulcers.

Live yeast is found in many commercially-prepared feeds, balancers and supplements and is useful for helping horses get more out of the fibre part of their diets. Prebiotics would be particularly beneficial, in addition to yeast, for horses that have loose droppings, poor doers and those that run up light after competitions.

## Gastric Ulcers

Equine Gastric Ulcer Syndrome (EGUS) was originally thought to be a problem that mainly affected racehorses, but research has now shown that endurance horses can also be affected. One study reported an incidence of 93% in horses competing in 90–160km rides. This suggests that it is not just low-fibre diets that are the cause of EGUS, but that the stress of competing is also a contributing factor.

EGUS affects the part of the stomach that has no built-in protection against the acid produced as part of normal digestion. Normally, saliva produced during chewing neutralises excess acidity, and this helps to keep a regular level of acidity in the stomach. The presence of feed in the stomach acts like a sponge to mop up some of the acid and provides a barrier which stops the acid from coming into contact with the stomach lining. When the stomach is empty the acid can splash around, and this is made worse when the horse exercises at speed. It is therefore recommended to feed horses a little fibre before they exercise to reduce the movement of the acid.

Feeding plenty of fibre is important in the battle against gastric ulcers. Some fibres are even better than others as they possess greater ability to neutralise acid. Research from the USA has shown that alfalfa is more effective at buffering acidity in the stomach than grass and the researchers who carried out the study recommend feeding alfalfa whenever cereal-based feeds are used to reduce the risk of ulcers forming.

# Suggested Diets for Endurance Horses

The following diets are examples that may help you to understand the levels of feed required for Pony Club Endurance. However, horses are all individuals so please do consult a qualified professional if you are uncertain what your horse needs.

Ryegrass is commonly grown in pastures and is useful for making hay.

**350kg PONY DOING TWO NOVICE 20–30km RIDES PER MONTH AND RIDDEN FOUR TO FIVE TIMES A WEEK. HOLDS WEIGHT EASILY.**

- 4.5–5.5kg of hay or pasture (dry matter basis).
- 1kg of high fibre chaff with oil.
- 350g of balancer.
- Electrolytes the day before, the day of and the day after the ride.

---

**400kg PONY DOING TWO INTERMEDIATE 30–40km RIDES PER MONTH AND RIDDEN SIX DAYS A WEEK. PRONE TO BEING A BIT OVER-EXCITABLE AT COMPETITIONS.**

- 6 –7kg of hay or pasture (dry matter basis).
- 1.25kg of high fibre chaff with oil.
- 500g of unmolassed sugar beet.
- 400g of balancer.
- Electrolytes the day before, the day of, and the day after the rides.

---

**500kg HORSE DOING TWO OPEN 40–50km RIDES PER MONTH AND RIDDEN SIX DAYS A WEEK. DOESN'T HOLD WEIGHT PARTICULARLY WELL.**

### Option 1
- Ad lib hay and pasture.
- 2kg of alfalfa with oil chaff.
- 1kg of unmolassed sugar beet.
- 500g of balancer.
- Electrolytes the day before, the day of, and the day after the rides.
- A digestive aid supplement containing yeast and prebiotics.

### Option 2
- Ad lib hay and pasture.
- 1kg of alfalfa with oil chaff.
- 500g of unmolassed sugar beet.
- 2.5kg of conditioning cubes or mix.
- Electrolytes the day before, the day of, and the day after the rides.
- A digestive aid supplement containing yeast and prebiotics.

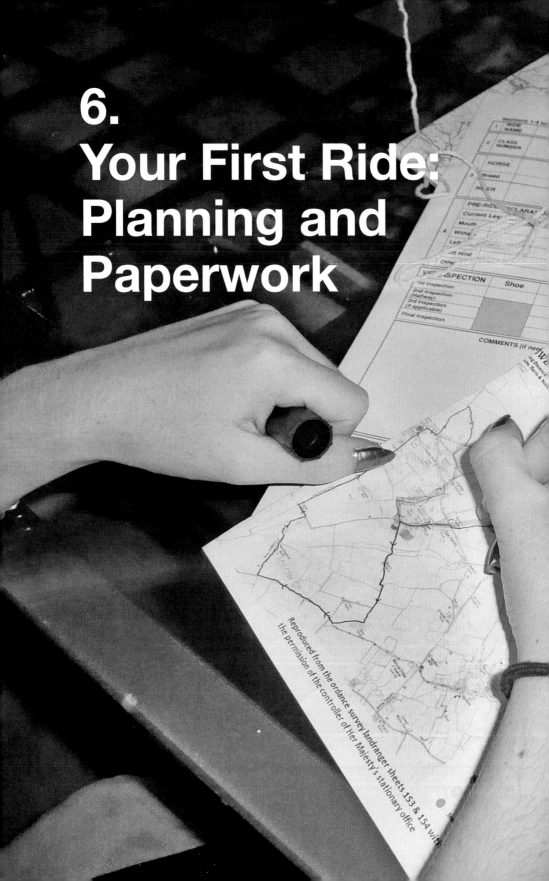

# 6.
# Your First Ride: Planning and Paperwork

# Choosing Your Class

First-time endurance riders should stick to a novice class, training ride or pleasure ride (PR). Pony Club Level 3 (Kestrel) rides range from 20–29km (12½–18 miles), and this is a good place to start for most riders. If your Branch/Area are not offering any organised rides then it is worth finding out the classes EGB/SERC/ILDRA have locally at the appropriate distance. All three societies' websites will show details (*see* page 152).

Riders who are very young, have young or unfit ponies, or who may be concerned about the speed required, may find Pony Club Level 1 and 2 (Robin and Merlin) training rides a better option. These classes have no minimum speed, and this will allow you to plan a quiet and steady first ride. Level 1 and 2 rides are up to 19km (12 miles) and are most likely to be run by Pony Club Branches. You should note that although EGB/SERC/ILDRA do offer PRs at this distance the rules are not the same and they will have a minimum speed you must achieve in order to pass (usually 8km/h).

# Entering a Ride

1. Complete and send off an entry form as required by the event organiser. The exact format of this varies between organisations but generally-speaking, a separate form must be completed for each pony/rider. (*See* example on opposite page.)
2. Almost all endurance rides have a closing date for entries one or two weeks before the event. Entries on the day are almost never allowed because the Ride Organiser has to allocate you a ride/vet time and you will need time to study the ride map.
3. Pony Club riders can enter some classes at EGB/SERC/ILDRA rides but the rules differ from Pony Club and from each other so it is important to check with the Ride Secretary or the relevant organising body Rule Book for full details.
4. If entering rides run by an organisation other than a Pony Club Branch, clearly mark '*Pony Club*' in the top right-hand corner. This ensures that you will receive any Members' discount on entry fees and are sent the correct paperwork by the Secretary.
5. Send your entry with a stamped self-addressed A5 (162 x 229mm) envelope to the Ride Entries Secretary listed for that ride.

*Previous page:* Reviewing your route map is an essential part of your ride preparation.

PONY CLUB

## ENDURANCE GB RIDE ENTRY FORM v7.8

| Ride Name | The College . E . C | | | Official Use Only | Rider Number | |
|---|---|---|---|---|---|---|
| Date(s) | 06/08/2012 | | | | Vet Time | |

**PLEASE NOTE that Associate and Non-Members must pay the Entry Fee for Temporary Day Members**

| | Class No | Dist | Type (circle) | Entry Fee | | Class No | Dist | Type (circle) | Entry Fee |
|---|---|---|---|---|---|---|---|---|---|
| Day 1 | 2 | 20km | CER GER (PR) £16 | | Day 3 | | | CER GER PR | |
| Day 2 | | | CER GER PR | | Day 4 | | | CER GER PR | |

| Horse | Hurricane | | | Horse Reg No | | Qualification (Circle) | | (NOV) OPN ADV | |
|---|---|---|---|---|---|---|---|---|---|
| Breed Society | New Forest | Age | 15 | Col | Bay | Ht | 13.2 | Sex | G (M) S |

| Rider's Name | Don Keigh | Member No | | Rider Qualification (Circle) | (NOV) OPN ADV |
|---|---|---|---|---|---|
| | | DoB if Under 22 | 13/7/1999 | | |

| Rider's Address | | Owner's Name | |
|---|---|---|---|
| 13 School Lane | | Owner's Member No | |
| Stapleton | | Owner's Address | |
| Nottinghamshire | | | |

| E-Mail Address: don@fake.co.uk | | E-Mail Address: | |
|---|---|---|---|
| Postcode: NN14 5DU | Phone: 01345 6794 | Postcode: | Phone: |
| | Mobile: 07971 432 | | Mobile: |

| Name of Crew / Helper | Crew / Helper Mobile No | Crew / Helper Vehicle Reg | Emergency No if no Crew / Helper |
|---|---|---|---|
| Mum Keigh | 07972 546 | 5654 KTW | |

**Dress:** A hard hat of PAS 015, BSEN 1384, EN 1384 or ASTM/SEI standard must be worn with the chinstrap securely fastened. If riding footwear without a heel is worn, a suitable caged front to the stirrup must be fitted. Competitors may not ride in Wellington Boots. Whips must not exceed 75cm in length. Spurs are not permitted.

| Stabling & Accomm (if applies) | Arrive Date | Number of Nights | Total Stable Charge | Type of Bedding | Total Corralling Charge | Total Camp/ Accomm Charge | Total Charge |
|---|---|---|---|---|---|---|---|
| | | | £ | | £ | £ | £ |

| I enclose: Photocopy of Flu Vaccination Certificate (if required) | | Tick: |
|---|---|---|
| A LARGE (at least 7"x10") SAE with sufficient postage to cover postage of Ride Information | | Tick: ✓ |
| Total Ride Entry Fee (Associate and Non-Members must pay the Entry Fee for Temporary Day Members) | | £ 16-00 |
| Late Entry Fee £10, compulsory if postmark of entry after closing date (not applicable to PR entries) | | £ |
| Stabling & Accommodation Fee (from above) | | £ |
| Other fee as specified in the ride schedule or other information | | £ |
| A crossed cheque, which is not post-dated, payable to "ENDURANCE GB" for overall total of | | £ 16-00 |

I understand that, save for death or personal injury caused by negligence, neither the organising committee of the ride, nor Endurance GB, accept any liability for any accident, damage, injury or illness to horses, owners, riders, ground spectators or any other person or property whatsoever. I understand that riding is a risk sport and that I will only compete if I arr fit and competent to undertake the class I have entered.
The ride is being organised under Endurance GB rules, which I will observe. A copy of the rules will be on display at the ride or can be purchased from the office at Stoneleigh.

| Signature of Rider or, if rider under 18 yo, Parent / Guardian: | Mummy Keigh | Date: | 1/7 2012 | Name of accompanying adult if rider is under 13 yo: |
|---|---|---|---|---|

There may be a photographer in attendance. In order for any prints to be sent directly to you, we will provide your / your child's name and address to the photographer. Please tick the box if you do not wish to receive prints.

Non-members please tick here if you do not wish to be contacted with further EGB information.

Members entering rides run by other Equestrian bodies must write 'Pony Club' on the top-right of the form. Membership and/or registration numbers asked for will usually be those issued to members of the body organising the event and are not breed registration numbers, passport numbers or your Pony Club membership number, unless so specified. In the example (above) of an Endurance GB entry form, the rider is a Pony Club Member but is not also an EGB member, so these boxes have been left blank.

## HINT

Make sure that you pay the correct postage amount on your SAE! It is safest to assume the large letter rate applies as the maps and vets sheets etc. which will be returned to you can be quite bulky.

# Ride Master Card

All Pony Club competitors are required to have a ride Master Card on which results are recorded. Master Cards can be obtained from Pony Club headquarters (*see* Useful Contacts, page 152). The Master Card forms the only acceptable record of your endurance riding achievements and is therefore a very important document. You are responsible for filling it in with the ride

Please note:
That this card forms the ONLY acceptable proof of previous mileage/qualification.
Please keep this card safe and present to the secretary at the start of every ride.

**THE PONY CLUB ENDURANCE RIDING MASTER CARD**

PONY CLUB BRANCH
WHADDON CHASE

NAME OF RIDER
Don Keigh          D.OB 13.07.98

NAME OF HORSE/PONY
HURRICANE

| NO | VENUE OR BRANCH | DATE | CLASS/ DISTANCE | SPEED KMPH | H.R | OFFICIAL SIGNATURE & PRINT |
|----|----------------|------|-----------------|------------|-----|---------------------------|
| 19 | THE COLLEGE E.C. | 06/08 2012 | 20km | | | |
| | | | | | | |
| | | | | | | |
| | | | | | | |

details (as in the example above) and must present it to the Ride Secretary when you check in, who will then complete and validate it. This will happen every time you compete. If you fail to provide a Master Card then no mileage can be claimed towards any awards and you might not even be allowed to start. This rule is so strictly adhered to for three reasons:

1. Welfare: horses are usually not allowed to compete at more than ten or so competitive endurance rides per year. The record card allows Secretaries to monitor this.

2. As rides are run by a variety of organisations it is not possible for Pony Club headquarters to verify results otherwise.

3. The rules for all organisations do have special requirements for junior riders of a certain age and for entry into some higher level classes. The Master Card records your date of birth and is your only proof of eligibility to compete.

A Pony Club Endurance Riding Master Card is issued for each pony and rider combination and qualifications gained on one pony cannot be transferred to another. This means that if you get a new pony you will need a new Master Card.

---

**HINT**

Pony Club Members aged eight and over are free to join EGB, SERC or ILDRA to access additional rides/awards/training etc. However, if you do so you will be issued with another Master Card for your pony and will need to hand in both at each event.

---

# Ride Information

The week before the ride you should receive your ride instructions in an envelope. It is important to take time to read through them *before* the day to make sure you understand them. The envelope will contain the following:

1. **Ride information**, including details of venue, directions and any special instructions for parking, water, crewing points etc. It should also state the official distance of the ride (which may differ from the advertised distance by a little but will be the distance against which your performance/speed will be judged on the day).

2. **Your vet time and start times** will also be on the ride information. Some rides may only give you a vet time, in which case the accepted rule is that you should aim to start within 30 minutes of vetting.

3. **Map**, likely to be a copy of the relevant Ordnance Survey map for the area of the ride. Often it may be no more than a photocopy with the route marked-out in colour. Unfortunately, this route-marking and poor-quality reproduction can obscure useful little details such as contour lines and it can be unclear as to whether you will be riding on a road, track, or on open moorland. Don't forget that steep climbs, downhill sections, hard tracks, soft boggy ground and a lot of gates affect the time it will take you to cover the route. If you are not familiar with the area it can be a good idea to get hold of an actual copy of the map and to check the route against it. Another useful trick is to study the route using an online mapping service which allows you to switch between map and satellite views. This will give you a good idea of the landmarks you will encounter.

4. **Talkround.** A few rides provide a written description of the route that you are to ride. Some will give descriptions of parts they consider particularly tricky or where routes diverge. If a talkround is provided, take the time to read it through and match up the written description with the features on the map. This will help you to recognise where you are going on the day.

5. **Vet sheet.** There are veterinary checks before you start and at the finish of all rides. The style of the sheet may vary (depending on the organisation running the ride) but the information needed from you will always be the same. There is a section for you to fill in with basic identity and class information and usually a section where you can bring to the vet's attention any blemish, scrape or irregularity of the pony's action. Make sure that your

name, pony's name etc. are filled in before you present the sheet to the vet (*see* below for a correctly-completed example). The space for the pony's starting heart rate, the midway vet check (if applicable) and the finishing rate will be filled in by the vet. There will also be sections for the farrier's check (if any) to be recorded, plus your final results and any penalties.

6. **Crew card.** Rides often provide a notice which your crew should place in their car to identify them whilst they are out crewing you. At some rides this is collected from the Secretary when you sign in.

---

**COMPETITIVE RIDE VET SHEET**

| Post Ride Vet Time | |
|---|---|

Sections 1-3 to be completed in BALL POINT PEN PNLY by rider before collecting number bib from Secretary

| | RIDE NAME | The College E.C. Championships | | | DATE | 06.08.12 |
|---|---|---|---|---|---|---|
| 1 | | | | | | |

| | CLASS NUMBER | 2 | DISTANCE | 20 | Kestrel | RIDER NUMBER | 19 |
|---|---|---|---|---|---|---|---|
| 2 | | | | | | | |

| 3 | HORSE | HURRICANE | | | EMERG CONTACT & VENUE | 01234 567891 |
|---|---|---|---|---|---|---|
| | BREED | ARAB | AGE | 26 | COLOUR | BAY | NO PLATE | SD17 6PC |
| | RIDER | DON KEIGH | | D.O.B | 13.07.98 | BRANCH | WHADDON CHASE |

**PLEASE TAKE TO VET FOR 1st VET INSPECTION**

| VET INSPECTION | SHOE | PULSE | ACTION | PASS/FAIL | TACK CHECK |
|---|---|---|---|---|---|
| 1st INSPECTION | | | | | |
| 2nd INSPECTION | | | | | |
| | | | | | |
| FINAL INSPECTION | | | | | |

| COMMENTS (IF NEEDED) | | |
|---|---|---|
| | FINISH TIME | |
| | START TIME | |
| | TIME TAKEN | |
| | HOLD TIME (IF ANY) | |
| | RIDING TIME | |
| | AVERAGE SPEED | |

| IF ELIMINATED OR RETIRED, STATE REASON HERE AND THEN STRIKE THE SHEET RIGHT THROUGH | FIT TO TRAVEL (ONLY IF ELIMINATED OR RETIRED) |
|---|---|

| PASS/FAIL | AWARDS | POINTS |
|---|---|---|

---

# Understanding the Map

It goes without saying that you will need to know how to read a map. You will need to:

- Find a grid reference (a specific point on a map using the numbers at the side and foot of your OS map).
- Read contour lines which tell you how steep the hills are; to recognise different features 'on the ground'.
- Identify how such areas as woodlands, rivers, groups of buildings, and even power lines relate to the map in front of you.

Time used in getting to know your way round maps is time well spent and quite fun, too. Every Ordnance Survey map has what is called a 'legend' printed alongside it. This is a list of the symbols you will find on the map and what they mean, as well as how to find a grid reference. Check them!

Double-checking your map and ride plan before you start is a very sensible idea.

It can give you a great feeling of confidence when you know exactly where you are at any point on your riding route. It is surprising how many endurance riders are hopeless map readers, but understanding

**HINT**

Using a highlighter pen, mark both the route on your map and also special features on the written description. You can then just glance at the instructions to pinpoint your position. If it says 'Go past black barn on the right and follow unmade road to a ford', highlight the words 'black barn' and 'ford' as key points to remember.

where you are on the map will give you advance warning of when you need to look out for a turning or possible hazard. Also do not worry about remembering all the route, but focus on what you are likely to see over the next ten to fifteen minutes of riding, and then re-check the map. Don't despair if you really can't manage the finer details of map reading because the course you are riding is always marked by flags, tape, biodegradable spray paint or lime, but it is best not to rely on this entirely as rain can wash away some markings, and vandals have been known to remove tape or signs. If you think that you may have gone wrong then it is best to take the time to stop, double-check your map and backtrack to the last

marker you saw if necessary. Remember though that endurance riding is not an orienteering competition so

Planning your ride properly in advance with regard to distance, terrain, weather and the equipment you will use helps both you and your pony to relax and enjoy things on the day.

as a last resort you can ask other riders, crew or stewards where you are on the map. However, you should be aware that crew and riders usually only focus on their own route—so if they are not in the same class as you their advice on where to go from here may not be particularly accurate! (This does also count as 'outside assistance' in competitive rides.)

The Pony Club's *Map Reading* achievement badge is very useful in helping anyone to gain (or improve) map reading skills.

## HINT

Before setting out on a ride, orientate yourself in relation to the course map. Knowing where the start point is on it will save a lot of stress and worry. Rotate your map around so that it is pointing in the direction you will be departing from at the start. Try to locate features you can see around you on the map—like a high hill, a wood or even a motorway. Remember where they are in relation to the start and to the course you'll be riding.

If you travel to a venue the day before a ride, drive around parts of the route in advance to assess the going, where various turnings are, and to evaluate potential crewing points. (Follow the route in the same direction you will be riding, even if it means crossing over your route.)

# Speed Ready-Reckoner

| Distance | Speed 8km/h | 9km/h | 10km/h | 11km/h |
|---|---|---|---|---|
| 1km | 7min | 6min | 6min | 5min |
| 2km | 15min | 13min | 12min | 10min |
| 3km | 22min | 20min | 18min | 16min |
| 4km | 30min | 26min | 24min | 21min |
| 5km | 37min | 33min | 30min | 27min |
| 6km | 45min | 40min | 36min | 32min |
| 7km | 52min | 46min | 42min | 38min |
| 8km | 1hr | 53min | 48min | 43min |
| 9km | 1hr 7min | 1hr | 54min | 49min |
| 10km | 1hr 15min | 1hr 6min | 1hr | 54min |
| 11km | 1hr 22min | 1hr 13min | 1hr 6min | 1hr |
| 12km | 1hr 30min | 1hr 20min | 1hr 12min | 1hr 5min |
| 13km | 1hr 37min | 1hr 26min | 1hr 18min | 1hr 10min |
| 14km | 1hr 45min | 1hr 33min | 1hr 24min | 1hr 16min |
| 15km | 1hr 52min | 1hr 40min | 1hr 30min | 1hr 21min |
| 16km | 2hr | 1hr 46min | 1hr 36min | 1hr 27min |
| 17km | 2hr 7min | 1hr 53min | 1hr 42min | 1hr 32min |
| 18km | 2hr 15min | 2hr | 1hr 48min | 1hr 38min |
| 19km | 2hr 22min | 2hr 6min | 1hr 54min | 1hr 43min |
| 20km | 2hr 30min | 2hr 13min | 2hr | 1hr 49min |
| 21km | 2hr 37min | 2hr 20min | 2hr 6min | 1hr 54min |
| 22km | 2hr 45min | 2hr 26min | 2hr 12min | 2hr |
| 23km | 2hr 52min | 2hr 33min | 2hr 18min | 2hr 5min |
| 24km | 3hr | 2hr 40min | 2hr 24min | 2hr 10min |
| 25km | 3hr 7min | 2hr 46min | 2hr 30min | 2hr 16min |
| 26km | 3hr 15min | 2hr 53min | 2hr 36min | 2hr 21min |
| 27km | 3hr 22min | 3hr | 2hr 42min | 2hr 27min |
| 28km | 3hr 30min | 3hr 6min | 2hr 48min | 2hr 32min |
| 29km | 3hr 37min | 3hr 13min | 2hr 54min | 2hr 38min |
| 30km | 3hr 45min | 3hr 20min | 3hr | 2hr 43min |
| 31km | 3hr 52min | 3hr 26min | 3hr 6min | 2hr 49min |
| 32km | 4hr | 3hr 33min | 3hr 12min | 2hr 54min |
| 33km | 4hr 7min | 3hr 40min | 3hr 18min | 3hr |
| 34km | 4hr 15min | 3hr 46min | 3hr 24min | 3hr 5min |
| 35km | 4hr 22min | 3hr 53min | 3hr 30min | 3hr 10min |

| 12km/h | 13km/h | 14km/h | 15km/h | Distance |
|--------|--------|--------|--------|----------|
| 5min | 4min | 4min | 4min | 1km |
| 10min | 9min | 8min | 8min | 2km |
| 15min | 13min | 12min | 12min | 3km |
| 20min | 18min | 17min | 16min | 4km |
| 25min | 23min | 21min | 20min | 5km |
| 30min | 27min | 25min | 24min | 6km |
| 35min | 32min | 30min | 28min | 7km |
| 40min | 36min | 34min | 32min | 8km |
| 45min | 41min | 38min | 36min | 9km |
| 50min | 46min | 42min | 40min | 10km |
| 55min | 50min | 47min | 44min | 11km |
| 1hr | 55min | 51min | 48min | 12km |
| 1hr 5min | 1hr | 55min | 52min | 13km |
| 1hr 10min | 1hr 4min | 1hr | 56min | 14km |
| 1hr 15min | 1hr 9min | 1hr 4min | 1hr | 15km |
| 1hr 20min | 1hr 13min | 1hr 8min | 1hr 4min | 16km |
| 1hr 25min | 1hr 18min | 1hr 12min | 1hr 8min | 17km |
| 1hr 30min | 1hr 23min | 1hr 17min | 1hr 12min | 18km |
| 1hr 35min | 1hr 27min | 1hr 21min | 1hr 16min | 19km |
| 1hr 40min | 1hr 32min | 1hr 25min | 1hr 20min | 20km |
| 1hr 45min | 1hr 36min | 1hr 30min | 1hr 24min | 21km |
| 1hr 50min | 1hr 41min | 1hr 34min | 1hr 28min | 22km |
| 1hr 55min | 1hr 46min | 1hr 38min | 1hr 32min | 23km |
| 2hr | 1hr 50min | 1hr 42min | 1hr 36min | 24km |
| 2hr 5min | 1hr 55min | 1hr 47min | 1hr 40min | 25km |
| 2hr 10min | 2hr | 1hr 51min | 1hr 44min | 26km |
| 2hr 15min | 2hr 4min | 1hr 55min | 1hr 48min | 27km |
| 2hr 20min | 2hr 9min | 2hr | 1hr 52min | 28km |
| 2hr 25min | 2hr 13min | 2hr 4min | 1hr 56min | 29km |
| 2hr 30min | 2hr 18min | 2hr 8min | 2hr | 30km |
| 2hr 35min | 2hr 23min | 2hr 12min | 2hr 4min | 31km |
| 2hr 40min | 2hr 27min | 2hr 17min | 2hr 8min | 32km |
| 2hr 45min | 2hr 32min | 2hr 21min | 2hr 12min | 33km |
| 2hr 50min | 2hr 36min | 2hr 25min | 2hr 16min | 34km |
| 2hr 55min | 2hr 41min | 2hr 30min | 2hr 20min | 35km |

# Working Out Speed and Time

There will probably be a minimum and maximum speed at which to complete the course. Check the rules for the class you are entering to ensure you get it right. If you are too slow you may be eliminated. For all Pony Club rides there is a maximum speed, so by going too fast you also could be eliminated or incur penalties. Check your *riding time* and mark this at various points on the map to give you an idea of your progress. It is important to work out how long it will take you to cover a particular section.

It is always a good idea to write down the maximum and minimum time that you have to complete the course, as well as the time you are ideally planning for, as this will help prevent you coming in too soon or too late and getting eliminated.

The formula TIME = DISTANCE ÷ SPEED will tell you how long it will take you to reach a certain point. *See* previous spread (pages 62–63) for a pre-calculated speed 'ready-reckoner' chart.

Distance can be simply measured on the map by using a piece of thin string to follow the route and then comparing this to the scale of the map. The Pony Club Endurance competition badge syllabus covers how to do this if you are unsure.

*Example:*

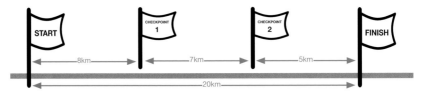

Suppose you have a ride of 20 kilometres from start to finish. There are checkpoints at 8km and 15km and you are aiming to travel at about 10km per hour (steady trotting, a bit of cantering). Using the speed chart overleaf, you can see how long it will take: two hours.

Checkpoint 1 is 8km from the start so it will take 48 minutes. From the start to checkpoint 2, a total of 15km, it will have taken you a riding time of 1 hour and 30 minutes. Note down these times on your map and also those for speeds of 8 and 12km/h over the same distances. This will then give you a good ready-reckoner in terms of whether you are travelling at your planned speed, a little faster, or slower.

When you reach checkpoint 1 see how long it has taken you. If you are on time, well done, but if you are behind time you will need to make this up on the next section. Ahead of your time means that you will have plenty in hand to slow the pace a little but not so much that you end up behind time. This is part of the skill and challenge of riding the endurance trail.

As a rule it is normally good practice to ride the route at a speed a little higher than your target average speed to allow yourself a margin in case you get lost or delayed. You can always slow down a bit over the last couple of kilometres to come in on the optimum time, whereas having to race for home will risk your horse vetting out with a high heart rate at a competitive ride.

## HINT

If you do not have a stopwatch but your watch has hands it is a good idea to set your watch to 12.00 at the start of the ride. This will give you your 'riding time' (e.g. if it is going to take you 45 minutes to get to a marked point on your map your watch will obviously read 12.45). This is much easier than starting your ride at, say, 11.43 and having to calculate 45 minutes from there.

**There are two levels of Endurance Competition badge.**

*Introduction to Endurance badge.* For younger or less experienced Members just starting out in the discipline. This badge will help them understand the basics to help them get ready to compete.

*Endurance* badge. For slightly older or more experienced Members who are ready to or have already started to compete in the discipline. It will help them to understand the rules of the discipline and what is expected of the horse and rider in order to be successful in a competition.

# Course Markings

Your instructions should tell you how the course will be marked.

- *Flags* are often used over open land.
- *Tapes* are usually fluorescent and tied to the left of the track so that they catch the eye on trees, fences etc. (N.B. To indicate a change of direction or junction where you need to slow down two tapes will be used beforehand and one immediately after.)
- *Biodegradable paint* is sprayed on fences or gateposts or on the ground for direction.
- *Lime (white powder)* is spread on the ground in the shape of an arrow to give direction, or across a forestry track to stop you going up that track.
- *Signs* may be provided at tricky junctions or where several different routes converge/diverge.

Be aware some rides are only marked at deviations from the 'straight on' route, rather than providing 'comfort marking' along the length of the trails. Tapes and markers (except flags over moorland) are not so frequent that you can literally ride from one to the other on the route. You must always look for markers. If you miss one and are unsure whether you are still on the right track go back to the last tape you saw and find where you are in relation to the map. It is not a good idea just to hope that by going on you will find another tape—check! There will probably be other mileage classes running that day and their routes may cross or be part of your route. Very often different routes will be marked with different coloured signs/flags; make sure that you check your instructions carefully so that you are following the right one!

Examples of three different types of route markings:
(above) arrow marking sprayed on the ground in biodegradable paint;
(opposite page, top) signs; (opposite page, bottom) tapes tied to the right of the track.

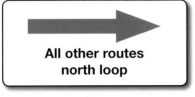

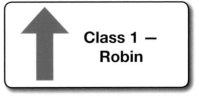

Be warned, however: animals are inquisitive beings and like to chew, taste or even consume orange tape; and canes and white flags make useful scratching posts. Markers that were certainly there last night may have been 'lost' by the time that the first rider goes out. Rain can wash away biodegradable paint and riders carelessly cantering over the top of lime markings can destroy them. Regrettably there are also people who delight in causing as much havoc as possible and think it a bit of a laugh to move markers. This is why it is so important to constantly look at your map. Keep your wits about you. Keep an eye out for landmarks so that you can pinpoint where you are. And don't just ride: look at and appreciate the countryside around you. It is likely that at times you will be going through areas which are usually not accessible to the public.

# 7. Your First Ride: The Day of the Ride

On the day of your first ride, it is time to put all the theory into practice. The night before, check that all your equipment and essential paperwork is together and ready—then to try to get a good night's sleep!

At the venue, the first thing you should do is collect your number and emergency stickers from the Ride Secretary and hand in your Master Card. The emergency stickers will be printed with the Ride Organiser's emergency contact number (which can be called by a passer-by if they find you or your horse in difficulty. You can also call it if you are lost, in difficulty, or see a problem that you

Don't forget to pick out your pony's hooves before you present to the vet both at the start and finish of the ride (and at any vet checks in between). You don't want to be eliminated just because he has picked up a stone!

think needs to be reported (such as damaged markers or an obstructed path)). Fix one sticker to your horse and one to yourself in places where they will be easily seen and won't fall off.

You should also check with the Secretary that there are no last-minute changes to the route. These are usually displayed on a board, and if there are changes, mark them on your map and check that you don't need to change your ride times or planned crew stops. Aim to allow yourself enough time after you arrive at the venue to deal with this and still make your vet/start time. If for some reason you are running late (unexpected traffic delays for example) contact the Secretary as soon as you can; most ride information packs will contain a phone number for this purpose. Generally, Secretaries will accommodate you if at all possible.

---

### HINT

Don't apply hoof oil before the farrier and vet checks as it makes it harder for the feet to be inspected—but the feet should have been picked out.

---

*Previous page:* And they're off—it's time to put all the preparation into practice.

There should be a marked area for the vet inspection. The farrier check and tack inspection (if any) will be nearby. Take a few minutes to familiarise yourself with the venue layout and make sure you know where the vet is and the start and finish points. Some venues are quite spread out.

Groom your pony and make sure that all your kit is laid out, as you should aim to start 30 minutes after your vetting. The more time you allow yourself at this stage and the more organised you are, the less likely you are to excite and stress your pony by rushing around. If your pony has a full mane then it can be a good idea to plait it into long stable plaits, thus allowing any water poured onto his neck to actually reach the skin and cool him as intended.

# The Farriery Check

Not all rides will have a farrier's check but most larger events will do so. If present, the farrier is not there to shoe your pony. His job is to check that the shoes are sound enough for the miles you are to cover. The farrier will need to sign your vet sheet to say that your pony's feet are in good condition so you need to present to him before you go to the vet. If he has concerns he may tighten up a clench but you should expect to be charged if he needs to replace or reseat a shoe. It is best practice to make sure that your pony is well shod or trimmed no more than two weeks prior to the competition.

If you lose a shoe on the ride you may be able to ask the ride farrier to get the shoe replaced before you present your mount to the vet at the finish. It is also sometimes possible to get the farrier to meet you on course. (N.B. It is usually permissible to present to the final vet with a shoe missing but you have to decide whether your pony will trot up sound this way.)

---

**HINT**

If you lose a shoe on the ride and can pick it up, do so. At least there is a chance that it can be tacked on. Most ponies should have feet hard enough to cover several miles without damage if you keep off sharp stones and gravel. There are also hoof boots on the market which can act as a temporary replacement and many endurance riders carry one of these with them as a matter of course. It is also good practice to keep a set of shoes on hand—with your crew, perhaps—which can be fitted quickly in an emergency.

---

# The Vet Inspection

The time for your vet check should be indicated on your ride paperwork. Take the vet sheet with you to hand to the steward. For safety reasons, and to make him easier to handle, it is recommended that your pony is wearing a bridle but he should not have on a saddle, boots or bandages. Take the reins over your pony's head to lead him and remove any martingale. You can walk to the vet with a rug on your pony but they will expect it removed for the inspection and trot-up. It can help to have a friend or crew member with you to hand over the vet sheet to the steward and hold any rugs.

There are often queues at the vet, both before and after the ride. Be patient and while you are waiting take care that you do not get too close to other strange ponies. The exact style and content of the vet inspection will vary depending on the type of class you have entered but in general you should expect the following:

1. The vet will need to listen to the pony's heartbeat using a stethoscope just behind the left elbow. Don't talk to the vet while he is trying to listen to the heartbeat. Try to be as quiet as possible and don't engage in conversation with your friends either. Often

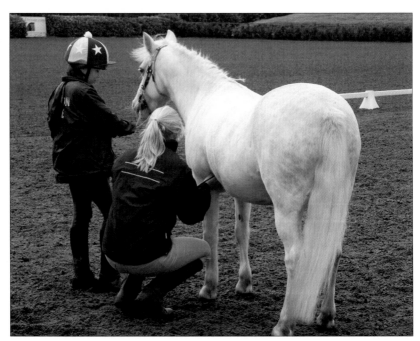

Your pony should stand quietly for the vet to take his heart rate.

even the best vets have difficulty in hearing a pony's heart, and an accurate count is vital. It is permissible to leave a rug over the pony's quarters whilst the heart rate is taken. (N.B. At Pony Club Branch/Centre rides it is permissible for an electronic heart rate monitor to be used instead of a stethoscope.) The heart rate must be at or under 64bpm in order to pass but after several rides you will quickly learn what is normal for your pony.

2. The vet will then note down any lumps and bumps which may be relevant. He will check that the pony's back and saddle are pain-free as well as legs and mouth. He will note the general appearance.

3. He will then ask you to trot the pony, in hand, to a marker approximately 30m (33yd) away and back again. This will enable him to check the animal's normal gait. If he isn't sure, he will ask you to trot the pony up again. All being well, you are fit to start.

4. At some events (for example, SERC-run competitive rides) the vet will then take the heart rate for a second time. This is called the 'Ridgeway test' or 'Cardiac Recovery Index' and is designed to show up metabolic issues. If the pony has coped well with the ride then the second heart rate will be very similar or even lower than that taken before the trot-up. If, on the other hand, the heart rate goes up more than 4bpm it can be an early indication that something is wrong. Generally the heart rate used for scoring purposes will be the first one taken.

The vets will be very particular about soundness and irregularities of gait. They will ask for a second trot-up, usually with another vet present, should there be any doubt. If the pony fails the trot-up you are out, eliminated from the ride. You do have a right to ask for a second opinion if it is not offered but apart from this you have no appeal against the decision. *The pony's welfare is always paramount.*

---

**HINT**

Many ponies can get a little stiff when standing around or travelling, so before going to the vet it may be worth warming your pony up a little after the journey. Often all that is needed are a couple of practice trots in hand to get him moving freely.

---

# Vet Holds/Halts and Vet Gates

As you progress to rides over 40km and attend more events you will come across, and maybe even participate in, classes which have required veterinary holds or gates which are simply a midway veterinary check and rest period for pony and rider. 80–160km classes may have more than one, some occurring at the venue and maybe some off on the course.

Your first experience of this will likely just be seeing a roped-off hold area near to the vetting lanes, and perhaps ponies being moved from here to the vet in front of you. The main thing to be aware of in such a case is that riders in other classes are not permitted to crew their ponies in the vet hold area. If you are entered in a class with a compulsory hold then you should prepare for it by setting up your crewing gear in the hold area before you go (*see* Chapter 8, *Crewing*, for more details). It is usual to mark out your patch with buckets etc. but take care not to claim too large a space—some hold areas are fairly crowded.

The exact rules for vet gates/holds vary but the basic principle is:

1.  You will complete a loop of the route and enter the hold area. The steward will hand you a card showing the official time you entered. You have a maximum of 20 minutes to present to the vet from this point but your ride-time clock is still ticking until you do so. This means that you should ideally present as fast as possible and is why riders in these classes are given priority at the vet. The Vet Steward will write your presentation time on the hold card and this will be your official time for finishing that ride loop.

Feed, water and crewing equipment should be set out ready at the vet gate, waiting for the rider to come in.

2.   The vet check itself will be identical to the usual start and finish vettings but the vet is specifically looking to see if the pony is fit to continue for the rest of the class. Any uncertainty about gait or metabolic stress is therefore quite likely to result in the pony being failed. (N.B. If the pony fails the initial veterinary check on heart rate alone then you are able to represent after 10 minutes provided that this is within the total 20 minute presentation time allowed.)

3.   If your pony passes the vet check you then enter the 'hold' period, which is usually 30 minutes after presentation (but can vary so it is important to check the rules of the class you have entered). Your crew really take over now, making sure your pony is rested, fed and watered whilst you have a chance to get something to eat and drink.

4.   The ride clock will start promptly at the end of your hold time so it is important to keep track of time and be ready and waiting for the Start Steward to set you off for the next section of ride. They will usually count you out of the vet gate: *10, 9, 8, 7... Go!*

# The Tack Check

Some rides (and *all* Pony Club competitions) also require a tack check. Before you present your pony, make sure that everything is in good order. The pony should be fully tacked up and you should be dressed ready for the ride, including any special items of kit that are required by the rules of the ride organisation you are competing with. (For instance, The Pony Club have a rule that you must wear a medical armband. Riders without one are not allowed to start.) Be careful to check the rules before you get to the event so that you pack everything required.

The Tack Inspector is not there to judge the quality of your tack but to check that it fits the pony and that it is safe. Make sure that your tack is clean, as it shows you take care of it, with no worn stitching on stirrup leathers or cracked and worn leather on reins or bridle. If you are using a martingale, check that you have rein-stops, and that rubbers on safety-stirrups are sound and that straps are tucked into their keepers. If you carry a stick it must be under 75cm (30in) long. Your hat needs to be to the standard laid down by the current Pony Club Endurance Rule Book and must be tagged.

You will certainly need a map case to carry your map. Tuck the strap underneath your bib to help stop it flying around and pulling on your neck.

# The Start

Get to the start, ready to go, in good time. At some rides you will have been given a start time but if not then the rule is generally that you should start within 30 minutes of vetting. Orientate yourself by looking at your map again, noting landmarks around you and how they relate to it.

Riders are usually started at intervals of one minute, but pairs and small groups can choose to ride together. Make sure that your crew's watch has the same time as the Starter's clock—which is the time you will be clocked at, not the one on your watch. It is best for a rider to use a stopwatch, or to set their watch to 12.00 so that it relates more easily to the riding time you worked out on your route map.

# The Ride

When working out speeds and times for competitions, bear in mind that hills and bad going can affect your speed, so you will need to study things like contour lines on the map and whether you are travelling on a tarmac lane or an unmade moorland track. The weather will also have an effect on your speed and performance. If it has been exceptionally rainy, the going underfoot could slow you down. In very hot weather, normally-soft ground will dry out and some tracks could become rock hard. If it is very hot, both you and the pony can become dehydrated.

Riders are started as small groups, pairs or individuals depending on their preference. It is therefore usual to have to wait for a few minutes before being allowed to set off.

*However—you are well prepared and are going to have a good ride. You and your pony are well up to the distance ahead; you can read your map and there are places for your pony to drink on the way; you had a good breakfast to keep your energy levels up, and have a high-energy snack in your pocket as well as a drink; you are wearing sensible, comfortable clothes, and your pony has comfortable, well-fitted tack.*

During the ride it is your responsibility to make sure that Checkpoint Stewards see you and note your number. They are there both for safety reasons and to check that each rider has gone through. If you do not pass every Checkpoint Steward in the correct order then you will be eliminated on the grounds that you have failed to complete the course. Obviously, if you ride past them at speed without giving them the chance to note your number then the same thing might happen! From the safety perspective it is reassuring to know that, if the stewards miss you, they will contact the venue and a search will be made. (N.B. You should ***never*** go home part way round, even if you live just down the road, without making sure that the organisers know. Safety is very important when you are riding out like this—not only your safety but also that of the people who might spend hours searching for somebody who just decided to drop out.)

At checkpoints, refer back to your notes and check whether you are ahead or behind your planned time and adjust it accordingly in the next section.

You must always be on the lookout for markers and be able to decide where you are on the map. Many markers are missed because riders are chatting away and not thinking about the job in hand, or enjoying a canter so much that they fail to spot double tapes warning of a change of direction!

A cheerful face can make somebody's day. It may be a tough competition but that doesn't mean you can't smile and thank someone who is kind enough to open a gate for you, slowed down in their car, or may even be walking or cycling along enjoying the countryside. *Be considerate!*

Manners on the trail itself are also important. Don't fly past other riders without giving them warning. Don't crowd other riders. Don't dawdle along a narrow track when there are people wanting to come past. Be aware that at many rides you will be sharing the tracks with more advanced riders who have to go faster than you in order to pass their class. They are not being rude or unreasonable in asking to pass.

It is a great temptation to shoot off when the going is really lovely, but a steady pace, up and down hill, eats up the miles and saves energy. Constantly changing pace, on the other hand, can actually raise your pony's heart rate. Aim to settle into a consistent speed as much as possible rather than dashing off at a canter then walking then trotting a bit and then walking again. On longer rides you will appreciate getting off and jogging with your pony to stretch your legs and he will appreciate the weight off his back for a little while.

## Problems on the Trail

If for any reason you are unable to go on, call your crew and ask for assistance. If you have no mobile phone with you (or no signal), wait for the next rider to come along. Get them to report the situation to the next checkpoint, telling them your number and what the problem is. The checkpoint will, in turn, relay the information to the start.

Never take a short cut off the route or rescuers may not be able to find you. If possible make your way slowly along to the next checkpoint, or the closest suitable point for vehicle access. If you are unable to move, use the survival blanket from your first aid kit to keep the injured party—you or your pony—warm. You can get very cold if it is a bad day and you may have quite a wait before help arrives.

If you come across another rider or pony in distress you *must* stop to ensure that they have the help they need before you continue your ride. In most cases they will have called their crew and just be waiting for them to arrive but if not then you might be the only person to pass them for some time. Even if the only assistance you can offer is to inform the next checkpoint of the situation do not underestimate how important this is. If you have to stop for a long period to assist another rider and you think it will affect your own ride results, inform the ride officials when you report the accident and they will usually make a time allowance.

---

### HINT

As part of your preparation you should consider undertaking some basic first aid training. Think through what you might do in a variety of situations before they happen, so that you can meet problems head on with a clear idea of how you would cope. Good preparation can take a lot of the fear out of things that may go wrong. The Pony Club offers two first aid achievement badges which you will find helpful—one for humans and one for equines.

## The Crew

If you are lucky enough to have a crew, you will have arranged places on the route where they will meet you. They will have a drink for you and your pony; water to slosh him down; or a bucket and sponge to cool him. They will know how you are for time and whether you need to push on or have plenty in hand. If it is really hot they might have a sponge of cold water for you to cool down with—one that hasn't already washed the pony. Most of all it is nice to see a familiar, encouraging face so remember to be nice to them! (*See* Chapter 8, *Crewing*, for more detailed information.)

## The Finish

As you near the finish, check your time. *Have you gone too slowly or have you left yourself plenty of time to steady down and start the cooling and unwinding process?* If you have enough time in hand then walking in from up to 1km away from the finish can help your pony begin to recover in preparation for the final vetting. Make sure that the Timekeeper gets your number and notes down the time at which you arrived. The Secretary will use your official start and finish times to work out the length of time you have taken to complete the ride and the speed you have travelled at. You or your crew may be given a card with your official finish time but if not it is important for you to take a note of this as you have to present your pony for the final vetting within 30 minutes of completion. Failure to present within this time will result in elimination.

After crossing the finish line, jump off your pony and loosen the girth. If you have crew they should be at the finish line waiting for you. Throw a rug over your pony's quarters if the weather is cool and a couple of slosh bottles of water over him if it is hot. You will usually then walk your pony back to your trailer or lorry for cooling off. (If you are at the end of a gated ride then it is normal to complete the final crewing in the designated vet hold area as well.) Now you can remove the saddle, and if the pony is hot, cool him off by sponging him down with cold water. Even on a colder day he will appreciate having the mud and sweat removed from his face, legs and under his saddle. Pick-out his feet and check for any small cuts or scrapes. Offer him fluids but not food. (*See* Chapter 8 for advice on getting a reluctant horse to drink.) Leave his bridle on as you will need it to trot him up for the vet.

Walk him round and cool him again. If he stales during this time it will help, too. You should eventually learn to use a stethoscope and be able to count the pulse so that you know exactly how well your pony is recovering. Keep an eye on the time and be ready to present to the vet promptly. Remember to feel the pony's ears and if he gets cold then you will need to rug him. Make sure he has enough rugs to keep him from becoming chilled but not heating up. It is very easy to over-cool your pony and shoot the pulse rate up again. You will learn by experience how your particular pony's body copes with the stresses put upon it.

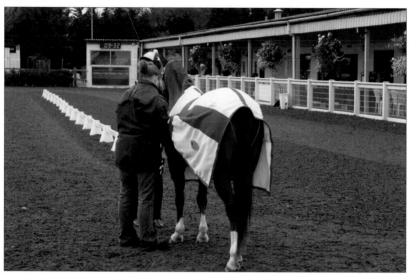

On chilly days the vet will usually be happy for you to leave your pony's rug on whilst the heart rate is taken—provided that the front is folded back or held up (as shown here). You will, however, have to remove it for the trot up so that it does not obscure the vet's view of your pony.

## Final Vetting

Final vetting takes place a maximum of thirty minutes after you cross the finishing line. Its purpose is to ensure that your pony has completed the ride in as good a condition as possible and the procedure will be very similar to that followed for the initial vet inspection. It is usually best to take your pony to the vet with its rug on over the quarters: if you don't do this, he may easily get chilled and his muscles could get stiff if you have to wait around. (You will, however, need to remove the rug for the trot-up.)

The vet will look for any new cuts or bruises and will check that your pony's back is not sore by feeling the saddle and girth areas. His heart rate should be under 64bpm. This is the absolute top limit—a single beat over this and your pony will be eliminated (or 'spun' as it is often called).

Your pony's state of dehydration will be tested by the vet pinching the skin over the pony's shoulder and then holding it for a few seconds. When the vet lets go, the time it takes to relax into position tells him how much fluid has been lost and whether your pony is distressed. (You can try this for yourself when your pony comes in from the field: see how quickly the pinch of skin disappears.)

It is worth noting that different endurance societies and different ride-types have different systems of marking and grading. You should always check the rules of the particular group with which you are competing and make sure you know what to do. It is your responsibility to do this, and it is well worth the effort.

If all has gone well, you will have completed the ride at your intended speed, your pony will be sound and his heart rate will have returned back close to his normal resting heart rate. Endurance is the only discipline where the veterinary condition of the pony is monitored so thoroughly. The challenge in the sport is to improve not just on your performance out on the trail but also to present your pony with a lower pulse rate and in a better condition each time, bearing in mind the weather and terrain which you have to deal with. This makes it a true test of horsemanship— and the understanding of your pony that you develop with endurance riding will stand you in good stead for any discipline.

## HINT

A calm crew and unfussy preparation of your pony before vetting will help keep his pulse rate down. People rushing about in a hurry, with high, excited voices and short tempers, and over-enthusiastic sloshing and cooling, won't help a highly-strung, excited pony to relax. Relaxing will help his pulse rate to drop. The ideal is that he should have returned to his normal resting heart rate within 30 minutes—this shows a good recovery rate and level of fitness. However, some ponies are naturally laid-back and take the excitement of the ride in their stride, while others may take a season or two before they settle and vet well.

# Aftercare

Now you have almost finished the day and are ready to go home. Your pony has had sufficient water and a small feed. You have prepared him for the journey home by bandaging his legs and rugging him up.

81

---

**HINT**

When you get your results, take a few minutes to double-check them. The stewards are all human and small errors do sometimes occur—perhaps missing a signature on your Master Card, for instance. These things are much easier to rectify if you spot them prior to leaving.

---

Bandages do have an advantage over travel boots in that they offer the pony some support for his leg ligaments, joints and tendons which have all worked hard. Many endurance riders also use products such as tendon cooling gel or clay routinely after long rides to protect the long term health of their pony's legs and aid recovery.

Before you leave, remember to return your number bib and collect your award, Master Card and your vet sheet—and don't forget to thank the organisers for their hard work. Be aware that results can take some time to be processed: the vet sheet has to be passed from the vet to the person working out the results (often referred to as the Technical Steward or TS). This has to be collated with your start and finish times from the Start Steward and then the whole lot has to be processed by the Secretary to ensure that you get the correct rosette and so forth. A little patience will be much-appreciated by all involved—by the end of the day it is quite likely that all the stewards are working flat out to get the results processed and dealing with a constant stream of enquiries as to how long it will take is only likely to slow them down!

Before leaving the venue, check that you haven't left anything behind and clear up any droppings from around your vehicle. Most venues will have clearly indicated places for disposal and it is not fair to expect the Secretary to clear up after you. Your pony will be glad to get home for a good roll in his field and to rest and relax. If he is stabled, check that he has everything he needs, then leave him in peace and quiet.

The following day, check him over for any injury or swellings. His legs may have filled, especially if he has been stabled, but this should reduce as he walks around his field. His hard work may be showing in a little stiffness and he may even appear to have lost some weight, but he should recover in a couple of days with rest and care. No doubt the rider is a little stiff too! A bit of gentle stretching or massage and light exercise in the days that follow will soon help you both to work this off. Needless to say, if you are at all concerned about your pony's well-being you should always consult a vet.

As a rule of thumb your pony should have a day off for every 10–15km you have ridden. It is, however, important for him to have a chance to stretch his legs and a gentle walk out may be beneficial, especially if you have limited turn out facilities. A good grooming will remove any sweat and muck left over from the previous day and will also give you a chance to check for tenderness on his legs and back. If his back is sore, you should work out why. Is the saddle causing a problem? Was your riding not as good as it might have been so that you rode heavily or were unbalanced?

Take some time to think about how well you did in the event and whether you were satisfied with the way it all went. Can you see where you made any mistakes? What have you learnt from it all and is there anything you would do differently next time? Check your calendar to see when your next ride will be and make a plan to keep yourself and your pony fit enough for it. With the benefit of experience and practice your next endurance ride will be even easier and more enjoyable for you both.

---

**HINT**

As your horse is having a day off, you will have plenty of time to give your tack a really good clean and check that nothing has been damaged. Time too, to check out the crewing equipment and make sure that it is all together for your next ride.

# 8. Crewing

Crewing can be quite a simple process—just a helping hand—or it can become a well-practised (and sometimes quite a complicated) part of a rider's strategy, depending on the ambition of rider and/or their crew.

Someone who may not be able to ride, for whatever reason, can get a lot of enjoyment out of endurance riding by becoming a valued crew member and novice riders can learn a lot from crewing for someone who is more advanced. Although not essential in low-mileage and pleasure rides, as the distance increases the crew can be a crucial factor in the success (or not) of a pony and rider completing a ride. Even for someone riding shorter distances it can be very reassuring to have a crew to see you off and offer support on your return.

The job of a crew member is to help the rider before the ride begins, to get the pony to the vet on time and ready to ride away, and then to meet the rider at points along the route with water for the pony and to offer refreshment to the rider. The crew member is also needed to help at the halfway vet gate/hold, if there is one; at the final vetting; and with aftercare for the pony and rider when they complete their ride.

To start with, all you need is a smile and to not mind getting wet from over enthusiastic use of slosh bottles and sponges. It is useful, however, to be able to read a map, so that you can arrive at pre-arranged points on the course at the right time. Crew need to know the route and make use of designated crew stops as well as any other safe and legally-accessible places you can find. Ride paperwork will often contain information about this but if you are unsure then it is usually possible to ask the Ride Secretary for advice. You should be able to tell the rider whether they are on time or going too fast or too slow. It also helps if you know the pony well and how he usually behaves so that you are more able to judge how he is reacting to any stress, and can be confident when holding him and handling him for the rider at vetting and crewing. Riders sometimes get a little stressed and say things that they may regret afterwards, so a thick skin is another useful addition to the qualities of a crew member.

*Previous page:* It's encouraging to see a familiar face on a long ride. As you progress, your crew will become a vital part of your team.

Properly crewing the pony at the end of the ride can make the difference between passing and failing a veterinary inspection.

# Suggested Equipment for Crewing

You can manage with a lot less on short rides, of course!

- Filled water-containers. (Five-gallon containers are quite heavy to carry so it is worth looking for something smaller.) *Never* underestimate the amount of water you need.
- Separate buckets for drinking and washing (although some horses actually prefer to drink the salty water left in the wash bucket).
- Sponges and sweat-scraper.
- Towels (for pony and for human).
- First aid kit.
- Sloppy, fresh sugar beet water (or the pony's preferred drink).
- Slosh bottles (with funnel or jug for refilling).
- Plastic crate/box (so bottles stand upright safely in a crew vehicle).
- Rugs—thermal, cooler and/or New Zealand (depending on weather).
- Headcollar and rope.

- Spare numnah, girth, stirrup leathers, reins.
- Spare clothing for rider.
- Drink and refreshment for rider.
- Copy of map and ride instructions.
- Stethoscope.
- Watch (which should be set at the same time as your rider's).
- Hoof pick and penknife.
- Thermos of hot water. (If it is a very cool day this can take the chill off washing-down water).
- Electrolytes (if using)—*see* Chapter 8.

# Before the Ride—Trot-Up/Vetting

The trot-up is most often performed by the pony's rider but a crew member may wish to do it for them. Whoever trots up the pony must wear the rider's number bib and, at the initial vetting, must also bring the filled in vet sheet with them. (*See* page 58).

It is recommended to have the pony in a bridle for the trot-up as you must be fully in control of your pony for both your own safety and the vet's. If you are a crew member trotting up the pony it is good to smile at the vets and say good morning etc. (nothing more) and keep

'Slosh' bottles are a convenient way for both crew and rider to apply water.

the pony under control. He should stand still while the pulse is taken and you should remain quiet to allow the vet to hear the heartbeat. If possible practice trotting in hand at home so you can do this really well at a ride. (For further details on vetting procedure and trot up technique *see* Chapter 7—*Day of the Ride* (pages 68–83) and Chapter 9—*Improving Your Skills* (pages 98–109)).

# Meeting Your Rider on the Course

On shorter or non-competitive rides you might not get to see your rider on the course, but longer rides will have designated crew points. You will need to be *quick, quiet, confident and organised.* You should try to avoid wasting time by chatting—have a good look at the pony and note any changes, small sores or a cut that the rider may not have noticed. Have a bucket of water ready and offer the pony a drink—but bear in mind that many ponies will not drink much before 30km, and even then they may not drink frequently (depending on the pony). Don't be tempted to try to force the pony to drink by sticking the bucket halfway up his face every time he stops. Your rider should make as much use as possible of water on the course such as natural streams, drinking troughs and so on, as some ponies will enjoy a slightly muddy puddle when they have refused the clean bucketful offered. Other ponies will only drink from their own bucket, and even then only familiar water.

Some ponies just love sloppy sugar beet swimming in a bucket of water. This fluid contains some natural energy sources, and if the pony will take it—feed it to him! It will also help to disguise the fact it is possibly not water from his own tap at home. Others will drink if bits of apple are floated in the water or a little juice is added to it. On longer competitive rides it may be possible to add electrolytes to the fluid for the replacement of salts, but only use these if the pony is used to the taste or he may not drink at all. It can take a fair bit of experimentation to discover what each pony will drink but your rider should be able to advise you of their pony's preferences so that you can have it ready and waiting for them.

You will need quite a large amount of water unless you are sure that the pony can be persuaded to use natural sources on the route. A lot will be needed for cooling the pony. Make certain that you have water, buckets, sponges and slosh bottles out before the rider arrives on the scene, and be sure that the rider can see you as he/she comes in. If there is time, sponge the sweat from the pony's neck, inside the back legs and under the belly. Offer the rider a slosh bottle to tip water from poll to shoulder on the pony to cool him. Fabric softener plastic containers make good slosh bottles; they are robust and have sensible handles and wide mouths.

Sometimes a crew member will walk up the route to meet the rider with a slosh bottle (so that the pony can then drink in peace at the crew point) or will hand a slosh bottle up to a rider so that he/she can cool the pony, throw down the bottle and keep moving.

Do not pour water on the large muscles behind the saddle unless the pony is moving off immediately. On a pony that is standing around the water may cause stiffening or cramping.

Make sure that the rider has a drink too—even if it is only a sip or two. Dehydration can happen inadvertently and can lead to errors of judgment, causing the rider, as well as a pony, to become quite ill (in which case it could be difficult to replace the lost fluids). Riders tend to think of their pony's requirements and not their own, but the problems of dehydration in the rider might let the pony down. If it is really hot, the rider will appreciate a cold cloth or clean sponge for his/her face, try to resist using the same one for washing the pony down! An extra sweater, waterproof or dry gloves may be needed in case the weather changes, so try to make sure there is something available.

# After the Ride

Don't forget to collect the timecard from the Timekeeper or, if no timecard is given, be sure to write down the finish time showing on the official clock. You should present your pony to the vet 30 minutes after this time, but don't wait until the last seconds before getting to the vet check. Keep an eye on the time and don't get flustered. Calm crewing can steady the pony, even if crew or rider are feeling anxious because things aren't going to plan.

After the ride your pony can be made more comfortable by sponging off the sweat where the tack has been, and under the elbows and between the hind legs. It is important your pony does not get chilled, especially if the weather is cold and wet.

Crewing should be done with plain water as soap can strip the oils from the pony's coat and affect its natural waterproofing. Your aim is to cool the pony and remove sweat, not to soak him to the skin by giving him a bath! On a cool day it can be important to put a fleece on your pony after sponging him off to prevent him catching a chill. You can leave a rug on him while waiting to present to the vet. Obviously, it is important to ensure that your pony is warm and dry before turning him out in a field when you get home; if it is cold and wet it is nice to rug up a tired pony for the night after the ride so they use less energy keeping warm and can rest.

It is not generally advisable to allow your pony to eat just before vetting but it is always better to let the pony relax by grazing than to get into a fight about it!

If you can, get your pony to stale, because it reduces the heart rate. Try walking him over to where another pony has just been as the scent may encourage him. It is possible to train your pony to stale on command— into a large skip full of straw for example.

Some ponies will roll when tack is removed and if a suitable spot presents, this will help him relax but it will temporarily raise the heart rate so you don't want to go to the vet immediately afterwards.

During the actual vetting, keep calm and remember that an anxious handler conveys worry to the pony and raises stress levels and heart rate.

It is good practice (and with some organisations obligatory) to keep a copy of your pony's vet sheets as this will enable you to carefully monitor his progress over time, as well as to identify any potential problems that may arise. If you join EGB/SERC/ILDRA you will be issued with a logbook or folder for this purpose.

## Cold Water Cooling Technique

Ponies that are very hot and/or competing in hot environments will need to be cooled during or after competition. They are then less likely to suffer heat stress, they will recover more quickly, will not become as dehydrated and are almost certain to perform better. You do need to use common sense when applying this technique: a pony with a thick coat will take far longer to cool off initially but could become chilled if soaked through because they will also take longer to dry. Conversely, one with a thinner coat may get cold quite swiftly in even a light breeze but will dry off more easily. You need to adapt what you do to suit both your pony and the conditions on the day. The *Manual of Horsemanship* gives more information on this subject.

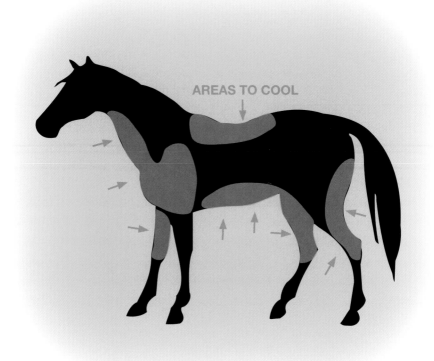

The best areas for cooling a horse.

The cold water cooling technique cools ponies using two of the three ways they normally lose heat—convection and evaporation. You will need buckets and sponges, a supply of water and small bottles (one/two litre size)—fabric conditioner bottles are ideal! You will also need a rug—a wicking-type fleece in cooler weather, a lighter wicking rug or anti-sweat rug and light sheet on warmer days.

- Immediately after the pony finishes exercising/competition the rider should dismount and remove the tack. Throw a rug over his quarters if it is a cold day. Take a heart rate if possible so you know how much crewing will be needed and start to cool the pony. Liberally apply cold water to all parts of the body including the quarters (this is where most of the large muscles used for movement are located and so is an area that gets particularly hot). Do not use shampoo or similar products.
- Do not scrape off excess water after each application, initially it

is more important to continue to apply cold water. Once the pony is fairly cool alternate cooling periods with short walks in a circle to keep the muscles loose followed by scraping off the water. Use the sweat-scraper, following the lay of the coat as you remove excess water. The walking and cooling sequence is important. The water sitting on the skin will warm up and effectively insulate the pony so it is important to scrape it off and re-apply. The walking promotes blood flow to the skin and cooling by convection; the movement of air aids cooling by evaporation. If you can, keep checking the heart rate to see how he is recovering.

• Stop cooling if the skin over the quarters is cool to touch after a walking period, if the respiratory rate is less than 30 breaths per minute or if the pony shivers continuously. A good guide is to feel the water coming off under the pony's belly—if it stays cool then you have done enough and should stop putting more water on, as a pony which is chilled will have an increased heart rate. Once your pony is cooled and the heart rate is close to normal put a rug (or more than one) on him if needed and walk him around to relax him. Do not let ponies stand still for long periods as their muscles can stiffen and this could be enough to eliminate you in those events where the pony has to be vetted.

• After your pony has passed the vet, take care to ensure that he dries off properly and is rugged up appropriately. Leg ice, clay or damp bandages can be used to help support his legs and tendons. He can be offered food and allowed to settle and relax but don't be tempted to just tie him up at the trailer or put him back into his stable or corral and ignore him.

---

**EXAMPLE**

This example illustrates the need to know *your* pony well and his heart rate range:

*'Thirty minutes after completing his first 32km, Dobbin's heart rate returns to 44bpm. This appears to be a good result but we know that Dobbin has an unusually low resting heart rate of 30–32bpm, so in fact his measured heart rate indicates a lack of fitness. When he is fitter he will return to 40bpm within 5 minutes of completing a ride.'*

Learning to take a pony's pulse with a veterinary-style handheld heart rate monitor (as in this picture) or a stethoscope is a useful skill.

## Using a Heart Rate Monitor or Stethoscope

A stethoscope (used in conjunction with a watch) is the traditional way to measure a pony's heart rate, but a heart rate monitor (typically consisting of a transmitter strap held against the pony's side and a watch-like receiver to display the heart rate reading) can be used to get the same information.

The heart is situated in the chest and is made up of cardiac muscles which work constantly to pump blood around the pony's body. The beating of the heart can be heard if you listen just behind the left elbow. A pony's resting heart rate should be around 35–45bpm but will vary depending on individuals and factors affecting fitness (such as age and weight). Fast or strenuous work may increase the heart rate to as much as 200bpm. As your pony gets fitter his heart rate will come down more quickly (the 'recovery rate') and this is the best measure of his improving fitness.

A veterinary-style heart rate monitor.

Get to know your own pony's heart rate and you will be able to judge how well he has coped with the work required of him. You should aim to have his heart rate return close to the resting level within 30 minutes of finishing hard work. The quicker the heart rate returns to normal then the fitter your pony is. At endurance rides you will be eliminated if your pony's finishing heart rate is over 64bpm.

# Vet Gates/Holds

Longer rides (generally only Pony Club Level 5/Eagle rides and above) may include a vet gate halfway, at which the responsibility of a crew to keep their rider and horse fit to continue is of the essence. Vet gate rules vary a little from one event to another so the crew must always be aware of how much time they have to work with for the entered class.

*Preparation is key:*

- When you get to the vet gate, look around to find where everything is, including the vet area, Timekeepers, finish area and toilet.
- Find a shady spot if possible—facing the vet gate so you can keep an eye on what is going on.
- Get everything ready in advance of when the pony and rider arrive. Set out your water barrels, buckets and feed for the pony. If it is possible, and you have enough spare kit, do this at the start of the day. Don't forget that you may need rugs to keep the pony from getting chilled, and maybe even a New Zealand or waterproof rug if it is pouring with rain.
- When the rider comes in, remove the tack from the pony and pick out his feet. You will have to prepare the pony to vet by cooling and lowering the pulse to the required level. Use the cold water cooling technique described on pages 91/92 but the aim this time is to pass the vet as fast as possible rather than to reduce the heart rate as low as possible. Focus on the pony's heart rate and as soon as it is low enough (usually below 65bpm) place a rug on his quarters and walk him quietly to the Vet Steward to hand in your hold card. If the pony is really fit he may be able to walk straight in to the vet with minimal preparation and you should certainly aim to present within ten minutes as this gives you the option to re-present if necessary.
- If you have multiple people crewing it is helpful to assign each

person specific tasks in order to get the pony and rider through the vetting and into the hold calmly and efficiently.

- The rider may want you to run the pony up for the vet so make yourself familiar with the procedure. Otherwise, just be ready to whip the rugs on and off the pony at the appropriate time.
- Note the time to return to continue the ride. (For more details on vet gate procedure *see* Chapter 7—*The Day of the Ride*).

At a halfway halt, it is pleasant for the pony if you have a clean, dry girth and fresh numnah ready for the second half of the ride. At the very least make sure that there is no mud trapped under the girth area, because if not removed it may cause soreness. It is also good practice to apply cool water to the tendons in the lower legs to prevent swelling and to sponge off sweaty areas and thick mud to increase the pony's comfort level.

At the vet gate, the rider should also rest, eat and drink. Even if the rider says they are not thirsty, make sure they are cool and drink plenty of liquids, as a dehydrated rider can be a danger to themself. Sports isotonic drinks can be useful to give the rider extra energy, and in some weathers a change of shirt and gloves can make them feel more comfortable to continue. If a rider doesn't need to go to the toilet during this break it may be a sign they are not drinking enough, so keep on at them to stay hydrated and remind them to keep drinking fluids.

Allow the pony to eat after it has been through the vet check so it can refuel for the next loop and to help it relax. Also ensure it has access to fresh water (or something like sloppy fresh sugar beet water if it will not take fresh water). Succulent foods such as carrots and apples can help entice the pony to eat and drink and help get fluids into them.

You usually have 30 minutes before you have to start again so there will be plenty of time for both pony and rider to rest before setting off again. It is important to keep hold of the timecard as starting off again late will affect your final time.

# Notes on More Advanced Crewing

As you become more involved with the sport you will realise the important part you play in the pony-and-rider team. Your attitude towards both of them will be the decisive factor in your success as a crew.

Your rider will rely on you to be in the right place at the right time with the right information. You will learn to judge how your pony and rider are performing and whether they need more back-up in the next few miles or should be left to run on. Eventually you will be able to advise and guide your rider through the ride as well as knowing just how quickly the pony's heart rate is coming down before the vetting. Your judgement will see them through.

On long, hard rides, when weather, terrain and stress have taken their toll on the pony, the use of electrolytes can play an essential role. (They are not necessary on short rides and should only be used according to the instructions for that particular product.) They can be mixed with, and offered in, water. However, some have a peculiar taste and the pony may not only refuse to drink the water containing them but could be put off trying another bucket offered with fresh plain water. (Ponies can be very suspicious.) Electrolytes could be slipped into sugar beet water if the pony is happy taking it. With a pony who needs electrolytes but refuses to take them in water, it is possible to put them directly into the mouth in a pre-mixed gel which can be bought in a syringe (like a wormer). Experienced endurance riders sometimes mix electrolytes with apple purée or honey in a syringe. Use of these products is not necessary until you reach higher levels of competition and of competence in judging your pony's needs.

Massaging the muscles of the hind quarters can have very beneficial results by helping the pony to relax and therefore lowering the heart rate.

It is often possible to volunteer as crew for more advanced riders and you can learn a lot about preparation, ride technique and pony care/ management by doing this. Even if you are not crewing for them, keep your eyes and ears open when you attend larger events—novice classes are routinely run alongside advanced classes and you can pick up a lot of tips and tricks if you are prepared to listen and learn.

## NOTE TO THE RIDER

Your crew is there voluntarily, giving up their time to run after you. **Try to be nice to them at all times!** You may get short with them as you will be tired and stressed out, but crewing is not an easy job! Try and remember to thank your crew afterwards and maybe return the favour one day.

# 9. Improving Your Skills

# Handling on the Ground

The importance of teaching your pony to stand quietly when he is being handled by the vet becomes obvious when you see the way some ponies behave. If the vet has to examine a lot of ponies in a short space of time he will appreciate one who, thanks to your efforts, meekly allows his heart rate to be taken and is not alarmed by the vet looking in his mouth and checking his back and legs. A relaxed pony will have a lower heart rate too, and that will give you better results in the long run.

When it comes to crewing, either out on the trail or at the finish, it helps if the pony is used to being washed and sponged. Most become used to it and appreciate it when they are hot and sticky but the day of the ride isn't an ideal moment to try washing your pony's back legs for the first time!

The farrier will also be grateful to encounter a pony who willingly lifts each foot at a touch and doesn't send him flying with a well-aimed kick. Time spent at home getting your pony used to being handled by strangers is not time wasted.

# Trot-Ups and Heart Rates

Veterinary presentations are part of the endurance job, so you need to start practising as soon as you decide it's what you want to do. Knowing how to trot your pony up is important anyway: you can practise when coming in from the field or whenever you ride. Just use a word or sound that tells your pony that you want a trot. Practise trotting in a straight line looking straight ahead and NOT at your pony. Your pony should trot calmly beside you, on a loose rein. The vet can't see if your pony is sound if he either refuses to move on willingly or if he is over excited, breaking into canter and pulling you about. Don't forget that trotting your pony up in a bridle gives you more control—just take the reins over his head and remove any martingale or breastplate.

To trot your pony up (as shown in the photographs on pages 98/99 and opposite), hold your right hand between a quarter and halfway

*Previous page:* When trotting up your pony for the vet you should run in a straight line, looking ahead, with the pony on a loose rein.

When trotting your pony up, hold your right hand between a quarter and halfway down the reins, beneath the pony's chin, and keep the surplus from trailing by holding it in your left hand. Do not wrap a lead-rope or reins around your hand.

down the reins, beneath the pony's chin, and keep the surplus from trailing by holding it in your left hand. Do not wrap a lead-rope or reins around your hand. If you hold the reins too closely under your pony's chin it makes it hard for him to trot freely and also might disguise any nodding caused by lameness. Give a little tug on the reins and a click or 'trot on!' of encouragement, then move forward, without looking back at the pony. If *you* trot, so should *he*. You are not permitted to carry a whip during the trot-up. Try to run at the side of the pony, near his shoulder so that you do not obstruct the vet's view. (In a competition, if the vet has not been able to easily see a free trot, you may be asked to trot again). Wearing gloves can protect your hands and give you more grip if the reins are wet but will make it more difficult to undo rug straps/buckles if you need to do so.

It is important to trot in a straight line. If you think that your pony might spook at something on one side of the vetting area then it can help to place yourself between him and the object that is worrying him. This may mean leading from the right hand side instead of the left.

As you turn round at the end of the trot-up make sure that you turn the pony away from you as you go round the marker. If you pull the pony towards you he will almost certainly tread on your toes and you will obstruct the view of the vet. You do not have to trot round the marker and it will usually give you more control to walk. Especially if your pony is older and a bit stiff he may find trotting a tight circle at the end of the trot-up quite difficult so the best advice is to come back to walk and then trot on again once you are straight.

A pony who trots briskly and willingly without undue encouragement will give a far better impression than one who is reluctant or misbehaves. (As a rule of thumb, at the end of a ride the vet is looking for your pony to appear as if he could continue the ride comfortably to do about half as far again.) Practise at home trotting your pony up from both sides so that you know what works best with your pony and that he will do as you ask.

Teaching your pony to follow obediently in hand will also allow you to get off and jog alongside or take the lead over bad ground when you will need to have more than just a few inches of rein.

Heart rates are also an important consideration and are used to indicate the fitness of your pony both pre- and post-ride. Having a stethoscope or heart rate monitor to use before and after you exercise your pony will help you keep track of them. You will notice that the heart rate changes as your pony gets fitter, but this is normal and a good measure of how well your pony is able to cope with the increasing workload.

---

### HINT

Practising the bottle handover procedure in a field or school is great fun and will make things simpler and safer on a ride.

---

# Sloshing

Ponies are quite often spooked when they first encounter slosh bottles being handed up to a rider, so it is important for both you and your crew to practise this operation. Start off with empty bottles at a standstill, then when your pony tolerates it calmly, try whilst on the move.

Sloshing on the move saves a lot of time at crew points and particularly on hot days can enable you to have a couple of extra crewing points without reducing your average speed too much. However, the crew member could be injured if it is not done properly, so it is essential that your pony is well-behaved and under control before you try it.

Sloshing on the move involves a crew member running alongside the pony, at his shoulder, in order to pass the slosh bottle up to the rider. The rider takes the bottle without stopping and pours the water over the pony. When the bottle is empty he throws it clear and carries on. If you have more than one crew member they can be spaced 20–30 metres apart and the process is repeated. This manoeuvre can be carried out at walk, trot or even a controlled canter. The risk is that the crew member can be run down by the pony and so it is very important that both rider and crew are clear on the correct procedure and have practiced beforehand.

Arriving at a pre-arranged crewing point offers a welcome break to both horse and rider; as well as a chance to check that everything is going to plan.

1.  Pre-arrange crew points so that rider and crew are all prepared and know what to expect.
2.  The rider should steady their pace and approach the crew member riding one-handed and with their preferred hand held out (to indicate which hand they would like the bottle to be placed in). Your own crew will probably learn your preferred hand but if you are ever crewed by other people you will need to make it obvious during your approach.
3.  If riding in a group, riders should travel in single file and at least one pony length apart so that they do not accidentally push their crew into the path of an oncoming pony. This also gives the crew time to prepare for handing a second bottle up to the next rider.
4.  The crew should fill up their slosh bottles—ones with handles (such as some milk or fabric conditioner bottles) are best—but the lids should be left off. A bottle should be held so that the handle is offered to the rider. (If crewing for more than one pony, a second bottle can be held in the other hand.)
5.  The crew member stands with their back to the approaching pony, watching over their shoulder. Just before the pony reaches them they begin to run parallel to the pony's track, holding the bottle up for the rider's free hand to grab (i.e. if the rider is reaching out their right hand, the crew member should run alongside the right-hand side of the

pony holding the bottle up in their left hand). It is dangerous to stand still facing the pony or to run backwards, because even a slight trip could make you fall under the pony's feet. Hold the bottle up towards the pony's withers as he may spook if it is waved at his head.

6. The rider takes the bottle, pours water over the pony and throws the empty bottle clear. It is important not to drop the bottle under the pony's hooves or in the path of other riders close behind, and it is a good idea to try not to hit a crew member with it either!

7. The rider continues without having stopped and crew pick up the empty slosh bottles before moving to the next meeting point.

# Working Toward a Goal or Event

When you have an idea of what events (not just the endurance ones) you want to do during the season, it is always important to consider what taking part in all of them will be asking of your pony. Don't forget that hills, flatwork, gates, showjumping, dressage, cross country, lessons and rallies are *all* relevant! If you have a weekly lesson, go showjumping or cross-country schooling a couple of times a month and hack for an hour or so most weekends, then it is more than likely that your pony will become fit enough for all levels of Pony Club Endurance.

If your events will be taking place somewhere hilly, practise riding hills beforehand, but it is worth noting that although galloping up them is fun, it won't make your pony any fitter! In order to train and utilise them for conditioning, walking and trotting are best. By doing this, your pony will learn to balance and use their hindquarters (which is where the 'engine' is), as well as building and toning muscles (including the heart) by sheer effort. The slower you ride up hills, the harder your pony has to work!

# Schooling

Just because endurance is 'out and about' certainly doesn't mean that you can skip schooling sessions. Your pony still needs to be balanced, able to maintain a rhythm and stay sound: schooling will help to ensure that you are working muscles properly and maintaining suppleness and obedience. Riders on the British endurance riding team are expected to do basic dressage as part of their training, and you could do a lot worse than follow their example!

The main task when schooling is to build muscle, create balance, smooth transitions and variation of pace. Obedience, trust, and learning to move away and off the leg, whilst remaining soft in the hand, are all important in the arena but how do they apply when out and about?

- *Long distances at one pace (trot)*: it would be easy to become unbalanced and one sided, so changing your rising diagonal equally is essential, in the same way as you would work equally on both reins in the school. A useful exercise would be to change your rising diagonal every ten strides and then make it harder by doing it every five strides—this is also a great fittening exercise for riders!

- *Going from a smooth to rough surface*: something like lots of tree roots can make a surface tricky to ride over. You could use a half halt to steady up or a leg yield to avoid obstacles.

- *Forests and wooded areas, puddles etc.*: especially when riding in a group, leg yielding your way through, changing your rising diagonal at trot or your canter leads will help you pick the smoothest path. This will also increase your pony's obedience and flexibility, and reduce the risk of lameness.

- *Teaching your pony to stand still when mounting* saves a lot of time and temper. It is bad manners for him to shoot off as soon as your foot is in the stirrup or your seat in the saddle, as well as being potentially dangerous. If you need to use a tussock of grass, a big stone or a gate to help you mount, he must learn to stand quietly. Even if a friend has to help by holding your pony's bridle while you get on, your pony will eventually learn his manners.

Try adding these ideas to your fitness programme. Schooling your pony regularly to be obedient, balanced and responsive will pay dividends. However it doesn't necessarily mean that you have to be in the school. It is part of your fittening plan and can be carried out on hacks too.

# Becoming a Better Rider

It goes without saying that a good rider achieves better results than a bad one and this is never truer than in endurance. It is easier for your pony to carry you if you ride in balance and rhythm with him. Simple adjustments to your riding style can make a huge difference.

Don't rise too high at the trot—*let it flow*. Check your stirrup length: you won't have to jump anything on the ride, and short stirrups can cause a lot of stress and fatigue on ankle, knee and hip joints. By leaning forward up steep hills you can free the pony's quarters and help him move forwards more easily—even if you have to hold on to a piece of mane while you do so. If you are riding downhill, ease your weight back a little and give your pony enough rein to allow him to see where he is going. Over the longer distances that you cover in an endurance ride and whilst training it will become easier for you to ride well, because if you don't it will hurt. Pain is a great teacher, and once both you and your pony are going comfortably together it means that you are riding well.

Good manners from both pony and rider are essential. Bad, uncontrolled riding, cantering on roads and general lack of consideration to other users of the countryside give riders and the sport in general a bad name. Remember the Countryside Code and be careful if you have to go through stock whilst competing or on a training ride. Sheep and cattle are only too glad of an excuse to rush wildly about and hurt themselves, and endurance riders passing their field can make them do this. Keep to the edges of fields where there are crops. It may look like grass to you but it is still a crop; deep and wet ground poaches easily, hoof marks will still be there weeks later. Organisers of rides have to do a lot of persuading

Keep to the bridle path and be careful to ride to the side of fields of crops.

landowners at times to obtain permission to go through certain areas, and careless or thoughtless riding may result in their never being able to use that route again. (The Pony Club runs a *Countryside Awareness* achievement badge which will help you learn more about these issues.)

Many of the places where you ride are used by others—such as walkers and cyclists—and they have as much right to be there as you do. Always give fair warning that you want to come past, and don't assume that they know you are there.

Consideration towards others also includes other competitors. Don't let the pressure of competition get in the way of sportsmanship or good manners. Smile and say 'hello' to people you meet and 'thank you' to anyone opening a gate. If you are riding a slow pony on a narrow track, try to move on—or over—so that faster riders can get past. If you are wanting to pass other riders, make sure that they know you are there by calling out that you want to come by. Don't just race past: you may spook a nervous pony and you could well get kicked; remember always to give other ponies plenty of room.

# Gates

You should be able to open and close a gate from horseback. The pony needs to halt and stand when asked, then move away from the leg (leg yield) in order to go into and out of the opening and closing sequence required to physically open a gate!

If you are unable to open and close a gate from horseback for any reason you may need to dismount. Make sure that your pony will stand still for you to mount. (It is good manners and far safer to wait for somebody who has opened or shut the gate to remount before you ride off.)

Gates are there to stop stock from escaping, so always fasten gates securely before you ride off. Ride organisers should check that there are no really bad gates for you to cope with, and they quite often arrange with the landowners to leave gates open for the duration of the ride. Check the markers so that you know which ones you can leave open and which ones must be shut. If you are riding in a group, take turns at doing the gates.

# Knowing Your Pony

The whole sport of endurance riding is based on a good working relationship between you and your pony. You have to know his capabilities. You need to know what is 'normal' for him, so that you can

Don't forget to thank anyone—steward or passer-by—who opens a gate for you.

tell if he becomes stressed, as well as how far and how fast he can go. You will become a better horseman the longer you spend in his company and on his back. He must have confidence in you as well as you having confidence in him. Together you will have a lot of fun and find out more of the meaning of true horsemanship.

# Time-Off and Fun

Never neglect the importance of taking time off. *Training training training* is no good for you *or* your pony, so make some of it fun too! All bodies need recovery time, so plan to do a little walk out or even nothing in the week following an event and, remember: providing you have mastered and worked hard at your base fitness, a couple of weeks off here and there will make no difference.

---

**HINT**

Don't forget to factor travelling time into your events and work, because travelling is—in effect—work for your pony! Some experts have suggested that the effort required by a pony to constantly shift his balance around whilst travelling in a trailer or horsebox is similar to that required when walking.

---

# 10. Running Your Own Ride

Riders in some areas may find that they cannot easily compete in endurance without a lot of travelling and in this case it can be helpful for your riding group or Pony Club Branch or Centre to run their own event. This is not an impossible task: a training ride does not need to be high level with hundreds of competitors. Novice distance classes can easily be run on the grounds of a farm or equestrian centre or as part of camp.

The equipment and personnel needed are fairly basic and once a suitable venue and route is established it can be used for future events as well. Financially, the event is relatively cheap to run and Branches who have run Pony Club rides in the past usually find that they are an excellent fund-raiser. You may also find that there are local groups such as BHS bridleways or EGB regional groups who will be very happy to assist you.

# Venue

The venue for an endurance ride is to a great extent likely to be determined by the availability of suitable routes in the immediate vicinity. (*See* guidelines on routes, page 118.) The facilities there can however be fairly basic. *Essential* ones include:

1. **A safe, flat area which can be used for the pre- and post-ride trot-ups.** This is usually conducted on grass. You may wish to rope this area off.
2. **A safe exit and entry to the venue** for riders, which is ideally not the same as that for vehicles.
3. **The ability to start the route/ride at, or very close to, the venue.**
4. **Adequate space and ground conditions** for parking lorries/trailers.
5. **First aid**—for Pony Club rides it is a requirement that you have a qualified first aider available in case of need at the venue and at any vet gate/hold (only relevant for Level 5 rides). At Pony Club level it is not necessary to have St John's/paramedic cover.

*Optional facilities include:*

6. **A water supply** is highly desirable, preferably a tap so that competitors can easily fill buckets for cooling their ponies after the ride. If there is no water supply at the venue you should advise competitors of this in the ride details so that they can bring their own.

*Previous page:* Running your own ride is surprisingly easy. The venue for your ride needs a flat area suitable for parking a number of lorries and trailers and very little else! As you can see from the picture, even a city-centre park can offer a suitable space.

7. **Toilet facilities**—a portaloo is quite acceptable.

8. **Refreshment facilities** such as a burger van or similar. The busiest time for this is once the riders return and after their final vetting has been completed. For the most part there are fewer spectators hanging around at the venue during the middle of the class than at other equestrian events. This means that even at well-supported rides the takings during this period are limited and you may want to advise the supplier of this.

9. **Photographer**—she or he will need to be out on the course rather than stationed at the venue. It is probably best to approach your local EGB/SERC/ILDRA or bridleways group to see if they can recommend someone who has experience of this type of event.

# Personnel Required

1. **Secretary.**

2. **'Vet'** and possibly **Vet's Writer/Steward**—Pony Club rules allow for the 'vet' to be any suitable nominated official. Heart Rate monitors may be used instead of stethoscopes. N.B. Check the current rule book to see what type of vetting, if any, is required for the level of class you are intending to run.

3. **Checkpoint Stewards**—how many depends on length/type of route. Your risk assessment (*see* page 121) may well indicate the best locations (busy road crossings, narrow bridges, difficult gates etc.).

4. **Start/Finish Steward.**

5. **Timekeeper** (may also be the Start/Finish Steward).

6. **Pre-ride Helpers** to mark and check the route and post ride helpers to clear the venue and any signs used on the route.

7. **Tack Checker**—for Health and Safety reasons Branches and Centres should ensure that Members tack and equipment is checked by a competent adult before they start.

Everything the Secretary needs to manage a Branch ride can easily be accommodated in the back of a horse trailer.

## Sample Job Descriptions

It can be a good idea to give some written guidance to first-time ride helpers. Examples for Checkpoint Stewards, Vets/Vet Stewards, and Start/Finish Stewards are printed here for you to use as templates..

## CHECKPOINT STEWARD

Your role is to check that each person on the ride passes your checkpoint safely and to notify the Ride Controller at the start point. The positions of the checkpoints have been chosen because there is some minor hazard, bridges for two, and a road crossing for the third. Needless to say if any rider has a problem negotiating these hazards feel free to lend a hand. The point of the ride is for the riders to learn to navigate and to pace themselves and their ponies. As such, outside assistance in the interests of safety is allowable. If your checkpoint has gates then opening them for riders is generally appreciated! CP4 has a particularly nasty pair of double gates which should be opened if at all possible.

If any rider/pony needs more specialist assistance please just inform control and we will arrange it.

### Notification of Rider Progress

Each steward must have a mobile phone and know how to send text messages. The ride controller's phone number (07XXX XXXXXX) needs to be programmed into your phone. Likewise, your phone number will need to be given to the ride controller.

All riders will be wearing a number bib, but may not pass you in sequential order as the different classes have different routes. To notify the control point simply type the rider numbers into the text message and send. E.g. '1 2 3'.
Your text will appear as CP1, for instance; hence we know that the first three riders have passed your point.

You will receive a list of ride entries to check off the riders passing your point. Once all riders have passed you please notify the control, and then you are free to return to the start to collect your respective children.

The target time for the 8km ride is between 46–60 minutes, and approximately double this for the 16km etc etc.

## VET/VET STEWARD

There are two distinct types of class at this event. Class 1 (Robin) does not require the pony to be vetted prior to starting, and these riders are allocated a start time. Classes 2–4 (Merlin, Kestrel, Osprey) require the pony to be vetted first and as such the riders are allocated a vet time instead and are asked to start within 30 minutes of vetting.

Entrants in classes 2–4 are allocated a single vet time per ride group in slots of 10 minutes. Riders should attempt to vet as close to the allocated time as possible and managing the queue to this effect is one of the Vet Stewards most important tasks. In the event of a large queue forming Mr Anysteward can be asked to provide extra assistance.

At the start all riders in these classes should hand the steward/vet a partially completed 'Pony Club competitive ride vet sheet'. If they haven't filled in the rider and pony info sections they should be asked to go away and do this.

The vet will fill in the starting heart rate and pass/fail on the trot up. Failure would be a heart rate in excess of 64bpm and/or obvious lameness. In the event of possible failure the vet should ask for a second opinion from the second vet or the Ride Organiser.

The vet may ask the steward to write the vet sheet for them in order to keep their hands free.

The vet/steward should retain all vet sheets after the pony has vetted.

At the end of the ride all competitors should vet within 30 minutes of finishing the ride. Failure to do so leads to elimination so it is vital that the final vetting time is recorded on the vet sheet. In the event of a long queue forming the final vet time should be taken to be that at which the competitor joined the queue and the steward should check competitors in and ensure that the time is correctly noted on the sheet.

The final vetting is identical to the start vetting. Ponies with a finishing heart rate of over 64bpm should be held for 10–15 minutes and rechecked to ensure that the heart rate is returning to normal. If there are any concerns about any pony's well-being then the on-call vet, Mrs Anyvet, should be contacted ASAP on 07XXX XXXXXX

Once the final vetting is complete the vet sheets should be returned to the Secretary ASAP so that awards can be worked out.

## START/FINISH STEWARD

There are two distinct types of class at this event. Class 1 (Robin) does not require the pony to be vetted prior to starting, and these riders are allocated a start time. Classes 2–4 (Merlin, Kestrel, Osprey) require the pony to be vetted first and as such the riders are allocated a vet time instead and are asked to start within 30 minutes of vetting.

An important part of the Starter's job is therefore to manage and record the actual start times for ride groups. Riders will usually start in small groups which are already arranged and indicated on the listing. Groups should have five minutes at least between them and will be expected to wait if more than one group arrives at the start at the same time.

Official finish times should be clearly stated to each rider in classes 2–4 as they are required to present to the vet within 30 minutes of this time. We should have a pair of linked clocks to use for official times. As ride groups do sometimes split once they get back to the venue please try to make sure that every rider in a group is aware of their finish time.

Your decision as Starter is final, in terms of managing the ride groups. You should aim to relay finish times to the control point as quickly as possible so that early finishers can have their awards before the end of the event.

# Equipment

1. **Rider numbers**—fluorescent bibs are best but any sort of cross-country bib is suitable. Card show numbers are hard for Checkpoint Stewards to see and are thus best avoided.
2. **Two accurate clocks**—one for start and finish times and the other for vetting-in times at the end. (Digital radio-controlled clocks are best as they avoid differences occurring in separate locations.)
3. **Clipboards** for Checkpoint Stewards, Tack Checker and Vet.
4. **Mobile phones** or other means of communication with checkpoints.
5. **Non-permanent spray grass marker paint, arrow signs or fluorescent ribbon** to mark route with.
6. **Rider Master Cards**—it is advisable to have a stock in case of new Members turning up without one.
7. **Rosettes/awards**—rosettes can be ordered from Pony Club HQ.

8. **Calculator** for working out results.
9. **Stickers** with Secretary's contact details—two per rider.
10. **Cones, tape, electric fence posts or similar** to mark out trot-up and vetting areas.
11. **Route maps** (ideally A4)—one per rider.
12. **Vet sheets.**

# Who Can Participate?

Anyone with a sound pony/horse can participate in endurance at Pony Club level. However Pony Club rules state that all riders must be at least five years old on 1 January and younger Members may be required to have an adult escort. You are advised to check the current Rule Book for full details and word your classes accordingly. You should also note that this is one area where Pony Club rules tend to differ from that of other

Even the youngest Members can enjoy participating in Pony Club Endurance.

bodies such as EGB/SERC/ILDRA and so some adjustment may be necessary if you are planning to run an event in conjunction with them.

Level 1 and 2 (Robin and Merlin) training rides offer a short taster class to younger/less confident Members or those with novice ponies. There is no minimum speed requirement, so even lead-reiners with walking adult escorts can take part and gain an award for completion. Levels 3–5 (Kestrel, Osprey and Eagle) are competitive levels which are intended to be more challenging. These are therefore primarily aimed at older/more experienced Members.

# Routes

(*See* the current Endurance Rule Book for guidelines on distances for the different ride levels.)

Level 1 and 2 Training rides can often be organised around a farm or equestrian centre's land. This offers a very simple way for Branches to offer some fun training rides initially. They could even be included as part of the activities at camp.

Realistically however, it is nigh on impossible to create a ride of 16km or more without it entailing some degree of roadwork. It is obviously desirable to keep roadwork to a minimum and to avoid major roads if at all possible. It is best for the route to offer at least some areas where riders can safely canter and circular/loop routes are preferable to ones where a long stretch of bridleway is ridden in both directions.

You should also consider the number (and difficulty to open) of gates on the route, as having too many will significantly slow the riders and, at Level 3 and above, put pressure on them to achieve the minimum speed. If you do have more than one or two then consider whether it is possible to arrange for gates to be manned or tied open. Other common hazards to take into account are poor surfaces, barbed wire fences, overgrown tracks, bridges, drainage ditches and stock fields.

For longer rides (Level 4/Osprey and upwards) it is important to think about places which are good for rider crews to use and if there are any places where crewing would not be advisable. These can be marked on the route map for the riders' information.

For ease of administration it is sensible to have the route start and finish at the same point—either at, or very close to, the venue. It also makes things simpler in terms of manpower and organisation if the routes overlap to some extent (e.g. the 16km route uses most of the 8km route as part of it). However, it is not desirable to simply ride round and round the same short stretch of bridleway, this gets very tedious and riders tend to bunch up. To illustrate—Anyhunt Branch ran their first rides using a single 10km route around the outside of a lake. This was then extended to 18km by adding an extra loop at the south end. Creating a 36km route entailed adding a further 18km loop to the north of the lake but this also enabled a 28km route to be run using the 18km north loop and the original 10km lakeside loop.

It is possible that your local EGB or bridleways group will have suggestions for routes and venues which you can use. It is also possible to make use of private permit only bridleway sections (e.g. TROT routes) by negotiation although this will usually entail a fee being paid by each rider. When you have found a possible route the first task is to measure it out on the OS map—1:50,000 is adequate but 1:25,000 can be useful if you are not familiar with the area yourself.

# Risk Assessment

Once you have routes of suitable distances planned it is of course necessary to ride or walk them in order to establish the suitability and safety of the ride. This should be done initially by both the Ride Organiser and the Branch risk assessment officer. Unfortunately the nature of this type of event means that it is not practical to do this by car as large sections of the route will not be accessible and in any case could look very different from a rider's perspective.

The primary purpose of the risk assessment is to check for unforeseen hazards (such as a difficult gate or road crossing with poor visibility) and plan how these will be managed. This should be done well in advance of the planned event as some hazards might entail a route change or additional stewards being recruited. (*See* overleaf for a sample risk assessment.)

It is not necessary to rewrite the entire risk assessment for subsequent events using the same routes unless there has been a major change of some sort, in which case one can usually just check the new part/ hazard. However, it is essential for the Ride Organiser/pre-ride helpers to re-ride the route (by bike or on foot preferably) during the two to three days prior to every event in order to pick up hazardous rubbish and check for fallen trees/fences etc.

**Date of assessment:** 28/07/2012    **Location:** Bxxxxxx Abbey

| HAZARD | HAZARD DETAILS | RISK GROUP | RISK LEVEL |
|---|---|---|---|
| Course | • General: course route, remote sections of the course, variable terrain and ground conditions | • Riders<br>• Animals<br>• Public<br>• PC officers<br>• Parents<br>• Property | • Acceptable |
| Course | • Traffic<br>• Roads crossed and ridden along are not busy | • Riders<br>• Public<br>• Parents<br>• Property<br>• Animals | • Acceptable |
| Course | • Overhanging trees | • Riders<br>• Animals | • Low |
| Course | • Gates | • Riders<br>• Animals | • Acceptable |
| Course | • Bridges between fields and water courses | • Riders<br>• Animals | • Low |
| Course | • Footpaths and pedestrian traffic<br>• Ride crosses public footpaths in several places, and runs alongside leisure trails for much of the route | • Riders<br>• Animals<br>• Public | • Low |
| First aid and welfare | • Adequate toilet facilities—yes<br>• Washing facilities—yes<br>• Medical and veterinary cover | • Riders<br>• Animals<br>• Public<br>• PC officers<br>• Parents | • Acceptable |
| Access to water | • Free access needed | • Riders<br>• Animals<br>• PC officers<br>• Parents | • Acceptable |

**Date assessed:**          27/07/2012
**Assessed by:**           Branch H&S Officer/Event Organiser
**Capacity of assessor:**  Branch H&S Officer/Event Organiser

Sample Risk Assessment

**Event:** Endurance Rides/Rally

| ACTION PLANNED | ADDITIONAL ACTIONS PROPOSED |
|---|---|
| • Course planned<br>• Course checked prior to completion<br>• Checkpoints on course<br>• Mobile phones used for communications<br>• Weather/ground conditions monitored<br>• Course marked at major changes of direction or potentially confusing points | • Riders and crew to receive ride maps and written route description and where needed an additional verbal briefing before the start<br>• Riders aged under 13yrs to be accompanied by a responsible adult |
| • Riders will use hi-viz number bibs | • Manned checkpoints at two points on the route |
| • Trim any brambles and significant branches | • None |
| • Gates are all designed to be opened from horse back and have been checked as functional during route marking | • None |
| • Bridges are all wide and well maintained. Low bridges over ditches/river | • None |
| • Paths all clearly shown on ride maps and the bridleway is a separate track | • None |
| • First Aid certificate holder at venue<br>• Veterinary cover adequate for whole period per Pony Club Health and Safety guidelines no vet in attendance needed<br>• Vehicle access to most areas possible | • Mobile reception check at all checkpoints and venue<br>• Inform officials of emergency procedure |
| • Access to water at the venue will be limited | • Advise all parties to bring adequate supplies with them |

**Date reviewed:**     xx/xx/xxxx
**Reviewed by:**
**Capacity of reviewer:**

# Checkpoints

Checkpoints, which are situated along the route and are stewarded, have three main functions:

1. They keep track of where competitors are on the route.
2. They help ensure that riders take the full, correct route.
3. They provide manpower/supervision at points which present a particular hazard (e.g. a narrow bridge or difficult road crossing).

Stewards at checkpoints should record the number of each rider as they pass and are allowed to offer basic help such as telling the rider which way to leave the checkpoint and providing water. In addition it may be appropriate for the steward to offer further assistance such as calling the venue for help with a lame pony etc. For this reason it is advisable to have stewards equipped with some means of communicating quickly with the Ride Secretary or other designated official at the venue. Mobile phones can be used or you may have a local Raynet radio enthusiasts group or similar you can call upon.

When deciding where to place checkpoints around the route you should aim to have one for approximately every 8km—although even a very short ride should ideally have one at the furthest point from the venue.

Checkpoint Stewards can be placed to assist riders and ensure their safety at particular hazards. In this case a difficult set of double gates out of a stock field.

Checkpoint Stewards should be issued with a list of all the competitors who are expected to pass their checkpoint. They should mark off competitor's times as they pass and return the sheet to the Secretary at the end of the event for information. A simple printed 'job description' can also be helpful for inexperienced Stewards (*see* pages 114–116. It is a good idea to have checkpoints contact the Secretary periodically to let the venue know which riders have passed them as this helps keep track of riders and means that awards can be given out to early finishers before the Stewards list is returned.

# Vetting

There is no requirement for ponies to be vetted at social, training and pleasure rides but it is good practice for both pony and rider. It also gives the opportunity to assess the pony's fitness and how well he has coped with the event. This can be as straightforward as a simple trot-up in front of a reliable adult, to ensure soundness before and after the ride.

For competitive rides and qualifiers a vetting is obligatory. The heart rate should be taken and the pony trotted up to check for soundness. The vetting should be carried out prior to the rider setting out and within 30 minutes of completion. Failure to present to the vet at the correct time can result in disqualification—this is especially true of the post-ride vetting where an extended cooling down period could significantly alter the result. However, queues can develop at the vet point and organisers should take this into account before disqualifying a rider on this basis; riders should normally be deemed to have presented to the vet at the time they join the queue. (*See* current Rule Book for full details.)

Ponies can be trotted-up in either headcollars or bridles but should be under control. For this reason, and for the safety of Members and officials, the use of a bridle is strongly recommended. Ponies should not be saddled or have martingales, boots, bandages or hoof oil on. The pony can be presented in a rug in cold weather but the rider would need to fold it back at the front for the heart rate to be taken and remove it completely for the trot-up. The person presenting the pony need not be the rider but must wear the competitor's number bib for identification. The vetting official first takes the pulse rate. A pulse rate of over 64bpm will result in disqualification and the lower the pulse the better. (In cases where the count is very close to 64bpm it is good practice to take the pulse

Vetting areas can become very busy and queues develop at times. At the end of the ride it is especially important to manage this properly so that riders are not unfairly penalized.

for an entire minute rather than for 30 seconds and doubling up.) The trot-up is over 20–30m and must be done with a loose rein. The vetting official should observe the trot up for signs of lameness. Lameness either before or after the ride is cause for disqualification. If the vetting official is concerned about the pony in any way they may request a re-present or a second opinion before the pony is cleared to travel home.

At Branch Rides the 'vet' can be any appropriate Pony Club official and an electronic heart rate monitor can be used to determine heart rate rather than a stethoscope if preferred. (These monitors are slightly less accurate than a stethoscope as they take an average of the rate of heartbeats, but are simple and quick to use for someone who does not have a veterinary background.) Veterinary students are often willing to undertake the vetting task for relatively little cost—you may even have some of these amongst your older/Senior Members. For Branches who are running a ride in conjunction with an EGB/SERC/ILDRA group training ride or similar you should check whether a vetting is being offered and arrange for a Pony Club official to be present if not.

It is common for queues to develop at the vet at the start of the event. In order to minimise this competitors should be issued with a vet time—gaps of 10 minutes between ride groups are usually sufficient.

If entries exceed 30–40 however you may wish to plan for more than one 'vet' to be present. Alternatively one can speed things up by either not vetting or not taking the heart rate of those ponies entered in classes where it is not obligatory to do so.

The vet will need a clipboard with a list of riders entered and their vet time. Each competitor should be issued with a vet sheet as part of their ride paperwork and they present this to the vet in order for the results to be recorded. The vet sheet is not returned to the rider at this point but is held by the vet until after their final vetting. The completed form is then passed to the Secretary in order for results to be worked out. (A copy of the vet sheet is normally given to the rider for information, along with their completed Master Card and rosette.) As the vet will end up with a lot of pieces of paper to manage it can be very helpful to have a steward with them to act as 'Vet Writer'.

# Vet Gates/Holds

**(Optional for Level 5/Eagle rides)**

At the Level 5 (Eagle) Pony Club Championships final the ride will have a midway vet gate or hold. The administration for this is slightly different from the finish vetting and as such Branches who run Level 5 classes may also wish to include a midway vet gate. Please note that this is NOT a requirement for running a Level 5 class, just an opportunity for Members to practice. Including a vet gate does complicate the administration and increase the number of helpers needed so Branches/Centres may prefer to run classes without one initially.

The vet gate would normally be located about halfway round the route. It may either be placed at the venue or at a different location out en route. All vet gates must have a first aider present and of course a 'vet' and Timekeeper. Crews will want to meet their riders at this point to help them and so it should

| Vet Gate Card | |
|---|---|
| Rider No. | |
| Time into Vet Gate | |
| **1st Presentation to Vet** | |
| Time: | HR: |
| **2nd presentation to the Vet** | |
| Time: | HR: |
| Hold Time: | 20 mins |
| Earliest time out: | Actual time out: |

be accessible and have sufficient parking. Ideally the vet gate area will also have access to water—if not riders should be advised on the ride instructions so they can bring their own.

Riders entering the vet gate are given a card which has the time at which they arrived on it. They then have a maximum of 20 minutes to present to the vet. However, during this time their ride clock does not stop ticking (i.e. if they take the full 20 minutes to present, that time is added to their ride time). The best technique therefore is for riders to present to the vet as quickly as possible. If they fail the first vet they can represent after a minimum of 10 minutes *provided that this still falls within the initial 20-minute period.*

The vetting procedure is identical to that described above for a finish vetting. The rider should pass their vet gate card to the Vet Steward when they are ready to present in order that the timing may be checked. The steward adds the presentation time to the card and hands it back to the rider. Riders who fail the vet at this point may not continue and are eliminated. Once the pony has presented to the vet the ride clock stops and the hold time of 30 minutes begins. This is an ideal time for both pony and rider to be offered water and food.

Riders should present to the Tack Checker (if present) prior to starting the ride but after vetting so that all their equipment can be seen.

The Timekeeper should ensure that the rider starts on time at the end of the 30-minute hold. If the rider is not ready to start on time the ride clock is started anyway and the time is added to the ride time taken. As the rider starts they hand their vet gate card to the Timekeeper who notes the time and then passes it to the Vet Stewards or Secretary so the details may be added to the vet sheet. (*See* Chapter 8, pages 94/95 and Chapter 7, pages 74/75 for more detailed information.)

# Other Pre-Ride Checks

At EGB/SERC/ILDRA national rides it is common to have a farrier present to check the ponies feet prior to the ride. This is not mandatory for a Branch-level ride.

Tack and clothing rules are a little different for Pony Club Members as compared to EGB/SERC/ILDRA rules. Branches are advised to have a Tack Checker present in order to ensure that Pony Club rules are adhered to. As a minimum, for insurance purposes, the Starter should be instructed to check that every Member is riding in a tagged hat and medical armband before allowing them to start.

# Paperwork and Administration

*See **Organiser's Checklist** on pages 130/131 for help with planning.*

1. **Maps.** These should be posted to the riders with venue and vet time details at least a few days prior to the event so that they can plan their ride. Endurance is not an orienteering competition! Routes should be clearly marked on the map, which is usually a colour photocopy of a 1:50,000 OS map of the area. It is good practice to indicate which OS map is being used as some competitors prefer to use the original map. Where a non-OS map has to be used then either the scale should be indicated or the distances between certain landmarks/ checkpoints etc. should be given. Any last minute route changes or information about new hazards should be posted on a copy of the map at the Ride Secretary's tent on the day.

2. **Ride talkround.** This is a written description of the route. It is not necessary to provide one but if you are very familiar with

the route it can offer an extra support to novice riders who are a little unsure of their map reading skills.

3. **Vet sheets.** Pre-printed sheets for each pony and rider combination that record all the details of the pony and rider and act as a record of their performance on the day. (*See* page 58 for an example.)

4. **Route permissions.** If your route is using public bridleways or crossing land owners land then it is appropriate to let them know what you are planning and ensure that there are no unforeseen difficulties related to particular dates or stretches of bridleway. If your route crosses major roads then the police should also be informed.

5. **Emergency contact stickers.** Riders should be issued with two stickers when they check in with the Secretary. These should carry the mobile phone number of the Ride Secretary or other official who can be contacted in an emergency. One is affixed to the rider and the other to the pony in case of separation! You may also wish to insist that all riders and/or their crews carry a mobile phone with them and advise you of the number so that you can contact them if needed.

6. **Vet times.** The initial vet time should be issued to the rider prior to the event. It is not necessary to advise a specific start time but this would usually be expected to be within 30 minutes of the vetting. Intervals of 10 minutes between ride groups for vet times are usually sufficient.

7. **Start times.** Except in the case of entrants who are not being vetted; it is simpler if these are not fixed but it clearly makes sense to start competitors in the longest rides first. This can be done by issuing them with the earliest vet times and simply advising them that they should start within 30 minutes of vetting. The Start Steward should not start riders too close together, or they will tend to bunch up. Gaps of no less than two to three minutes between ride groups are advisable, with groups of no more than four to five riders starting together. It is essential that the Start Steward accurately records the actual start and finish time of each rider but at Branch level simply ensuring that the same watch or clock is used for the whole event is sufficient.

8. **Route marking.** This should be done with temporary grass spray

paint, arrow signs or tapes. Paint or arrows are much easier for the riders to follow as you can indicate direction. Paint is also less likely to be moved by accident. Printed signs can be helpful at points where several routes converge to ensure that riders take the correct turn. In general it is only necessary to mark changes of direction or places where riders might get confused but arrows every so often, even along a straight section, are very reassuring to competitors. If using fluorescent tapes the accepted protocol is that they are hung along the left hand side of the route on trees and fences; at a height easy to see from horseback. Changes of direction or places where routes cross and/or riders need to take care are indicated by two tapes hung together followed by a single tape immediately after the junction/hazard.

9. **Working out ride speeds**. Use the formula (SPEED = DISTANCE ÷ TIME) to work out competitors ride speeds or alternatively *see* pages 62–63 for a chart which can be used instead.

10. **Master Cards.** It is very important that you complete and sign the rider's Master Card and give it back to them at the end of the ride. The riders should be encouraged to fill in the ride/class details before they hand the card in to you as it saves you a remarkable amount of time at the end of the ride. (*See* page 56 for an example).

11. **Placings.** The spirit of endurance riding is that 'to complete is to win'. At most Branch/Centre events it is anticipated that riders will be given awards based on their individual performance/class rather than in comparison to other riders. However, if you wished to run a more competitive event, perhaps with teams, then performance formula can be used to place riders first to sixth etc. (The greater the number of points the higher the placing.) Please note that this is not recommended for Level 1 and 2 rides which have no minimum speed and are designed to be used as non-competitive training rides.

## FORMULA FOR CALCULATING PERFORMANCE

$$\text{POINTS} = \frac{(2 \times \text{SPEED} - \text{MINIMUM SPEED FOR THE CLASS}) \times 100}{\text{FINAL PULSE}}$$

# Organisers' Checklist

**1.** **Route**

a. Map

b. Notify authorities etc. as needed

c. Trim overhanging branches or clear obstructions etc. H & S.

d. Mark out with spray/tape

e. Venue signs

f. Instructions for competitors on how to get to venue

**2.** **Dates (opening, closing, sending out pack)**

**3.** **Entry forms**

**4.** **List of entrants**

**5.** **Logistics information for competitors**

Parking, facilities, any special instructions etc.

**6.** **Talkround (possible)**

**7.** **Health and safety**

a. Low hanging branches (trim first)

b. Impassable gates

c. Livestock

d. Building sites

e. Road crossings

f. Copy of Pony Club insurance

g. Signs to pin up (standard at Pony Club events)

8.      **Team**
a.      Secretary
b.      Health and Safety Officer
c.      First Aider (at venue/vet gate)
d.      Stewards
e.      Starter
f.      Finisher
g.      Vet/appointed person for heart rate
h.      Vet Steward
i.      Route Markers
j.      Tack Checker

9.      **Organisation of Checkpoint Stewards**
a.      At least one checkpoint on every ride
b.      Steward instructions (child drop-off, route correct, check-off riders, help for rider so preferably accessible from road)
c.      Rider list
d.      Dedicated mobile number/use of radios

10.     **Radios/mobile phones for communication**

11.     **Vet sheets and vet gate cards (if required)**

12.     **Number bibs**

13.     **Rosettes/awards**

14.     **Spare Master Cards**

15.     **Emergency number stickers**

16.     **Catering**

17.     **Toilets**

18.     **Photographer**

# 11. Trekking

The word 'trekking' may bring to mind a convoy of bored ponies trailing along at a minimal pace, carrying novices or non-riders, but it can be so much more than this. In fact, it can inspire a burning ambition to learn to ride and to become a real horseman!

Throughout the course of history, there have been a number of legendary treks. Between 1925 and 1927 a Swiss-born, Argentine professor, writer, and adventurer called A.F. Tschiffely rode from Buenos Aires to Washington D.C.—a distance of 10,000 miles! Many people at the time said that it couldn't be done. It remains an astonishing feat of horsemanship.

Matching Tschiffely's epic journey might be a bit ambitious but spending several days with friends riding in the countryside and camping out at night can be enormous fun and well within the capabilities of most Members and the average pony. It may be that your Branch organises a trek for Members, or it could be just a group of friends planning a day or more away. It could be three or four friends or it could be a larger group. It is not advisable to go alone, as quite apart from the safety aspect horses and ponies are sociable animals and prefer not to be on their own. It is quite remarkable how horses can form a bond after several days spent riding together.

Trekking centres offer a range of activities from riding in a 'nose-to-tail' novice string to more adventurous, faster rides, taking your own or a hired horse on a pre-arranged, carefully planned ride of several days. You can find suitable establishments through advertisements in magazines, or from the BHS or by personal recommendation—the latter is best.

Your trek should be like a holiday, it is a non-competitive and social occupation and with a group of friends you can enjoy a real adventure. One difference between endurance riding and trekking is the time it takes to make the journey. When you are doing an endurance ride there is a need to finish within a certain time if you are to gain maximum points. On a trek there is time to stop, enjoy (perhaps photograph) the view, time to enjoy a leisurely picnic, time to splash in the stream as you cross or pop over an inviting log. You can rest your horse and let him graze at a suitable spot, there maybe an opportunity to 'sightsee' on the way, time to chat as you go and time to stop for an ice cream if the fancy takes you. There is no better way to explore the British countryside.

*Previous page:* Britain has a maze of bridleways which you can explore by planning your own pony trek.

It makes life easier if your ponies will stand quietly together when tied up.

Trekking can take you to places you have never been before and gives you time to enjoy the scenery as you go.

Sometimes the things you meet on a trek can come as quite a surprise! (Milton Keynes really *does* have a herd of concrete cows.)

135

# Your Own Trek

Finding your own way, working out how long it will take, knowing what equipment to carry and having a fit horse to share it with is a real journey of adventure. Britain offers a maze of bridleways, many of which are linked together to make long distance riding routes. There are various specialist publications available which list places offering bed and breakfast for horses and riders. These will give you ideas for routes—or you can work out your own, using Ordnance Survey maps. Remember, though, that because a path is marked on the map it doesn't always mean that you can physically negotiate it. Local bridleway groups may be able to give you advice. Lots of research is needed before you embark on a lengthy trek. It may be you can work out an enjoyable trek to start with by joining up local routes that you already know, or together with friends in a neighbouring area, you can work out a route that crosses country you are all familiar with.

# Safety

Just like in every other equestrian discipline, it is essential that you take proper account of all the safety aspects of your planned trek:

1. **Route**. Amount of roadwork and possible traffic-related problems. Natural hazards of terrain—boggy or stony going, an unexpected route change (due to a tree fallen across the path for instance) very steep slope, suitable river crossings.
2. **Your pony.** He should be comfortable, sound and sensible to ride and it is much nicer if he is willing to be tied up.
3. **Equipment.** Everything must fit properly and be in good, sound condition. Make sure that you can easily put up any tent you will be carrying with you. It is a good idea to practise putting it up and taking it down before you go.

---

**HINT**

Although most of your route will not be on the road, it is still a good idea to wear a high-visibility jacket or waistcoat. It is possible to purchase tee shirts in 'hi-viz' material if the weather is warm. If there was to be any sort of incident and you needed help for you or your horse, then wearing something that is easy to see will enable emergency services or a vet to find you more quickly.

---

Corralling offers a cheap and safe option for accommodating ponies overnight.

4.  **Suitability of companions.** You should all be capable horsemen and women and your horses should all get along. It is a good idea to take short practice rides together with your intended companions. Once horses have got to know each other they usually form a 'herd' quite naturally themselves. If there is a problem the horses will usually stay together. Of course this is also helpful if they are to be turned out together at night.

There should be no fewer than four in your group; in the event of trouble, one person can go for help; one can act as horse-holder and one can remain with the injured rider. As well as safety in numbers, there is also safety in good pre-planning. Six is the maximum number for riding as a group safely on all but the quietest roads without having to make arrangements for warning signs, back-up personnel and/or a vehicle with hazard lights to accompany the group. You should all be able to work as a team and each should know how to read a map. Always leave a route-plan with a parent or other responsible person in case of emergency.

# Preparation for Your Trek

Preparation for your trek is similar to that for endurance, in as much as you and your horse must be fit enough to cover the distance planned for each day, but as you plan your route you will also need to arrange overnight stops for you and your horse. You must also be able to ensure your horse has adequate suitable feed on route. Your tack and equipment must fit and be comfortable and you will need some sort of saddlebag to carry things you need with you. A backpack or rucksack is not suitable and will be very uncomfortable for you—and the horse, after a few miles.

Your usual tack will be quite suitable, but it is helpful if your saddle has sufficient D-rings. Modern saddles usually have them in the front and possibly on one side at the back. You may need them on both sides to balance your pack. Needless to say, your saddle must fit your horse, allowing freedom of shoulder movement and distributing your weight as evenly as possible over his back. It must be comfortable, as you are going to be in it a long time—even though you will be getting off and walking occasionally. You could invest in a 'seat saver' either of sheepskin or a 'gel pad' type. These slip over the seat of your saddle and are attached by tape or elastic.

A good-quality numnah will help make your horse more comfortable, but he may get very sweaty, especially if the weather is hot. You will need to be able to dry and brush off your numnah or make arrangements to wash and dry, or have a replacement at your overnight stop in order to prevent a sore back.

You will need a headcollar under your bridle and you should carry a rope, attached to the saddle or around the horse's neck. Combination bridles are ideal for trekking as you need only unclip the bit hanger from the D-rings on the bridle to have a headcollar; if you are thinking of more than one trekking adventure it may well be a good thing to consider. They come in webbing or BioThane (a plastic-coated, washable material which is very strong and available in lots of colours: but remember that for Pony Club disciplines other than endurance you will be expected to have a black or brown bridle). A hunting-style breastplate is something else to consider. In some areas of Wales and on Exmoor for instance, it is strongly recommended for endurance rides and trekking due to the steep gradient of some of the byways and paths.

Remember, unlike other disciplines you are going to be in the saddle for many hours a day and perhaps for several days at a time, so it is very important for all your tack to be soft and supple, and it must fit well in order to avoid galls and sores.

You may need to carry an extra layer or coat, or perhaps swimwear and a towel; you will almost certainly need a drink and picnic food,

At the end of an exciting day trekking, camping with your pony and your Pony Club friends can be a lot of fun!

even if you are not camping out. You could use saddlebags that go each side behind the saddle, or a cantle bag which attaches to the back of the saddle. If you are not carrying a lot, numnahs are available with pockets behind the saddle flap—big enough for picnics or a small fold-up cagoule. Endurance suppliers have bottle bags available to purchase which clip onto the saddle D-rings and girth strap, and/or a small Nylon belt bag could be fixed through your breastplate strap (on the part that goes between the neck strap and the saddle D-ring). With a little ingenuity it should not be too difficult to carry all you need.

### HINT

You should carry some basic items, such as mobile phone and first-aid on your person—perhaps in a pocket or a small bum bag. If you do have an unfortunate fall, it is no good needing something only to discover it is still in your saddlebag and your horse has trotted some way off.

Whichever way you decide to carry your baggage, before you set off make sure that your horse is used to carrying a strange load safely. The weight must be evenly distributed and must not bang about. If you are planning to camp out you will have to consider the extra equipment needed and decide how you are going to carry it. A pack pony may seem like a good idea in theory but leading the extra horse can be a trial and a hazard. Better to think logically about equipment that can be shared and try to distribute the extra weight between you.

If you are camping out a good alternative is another person meeting you all at your overnight stop with your equipment or possibly, if one of you is arranging to check your route before you go you could drop off equipment and/or feeds at suitable places.

# Suggested Pack List

Riders should take with them a small first aid kit (*see* Chapter 3—*Equipment* for a suggested list of what it should contain) and it should be carried on their person because if the worst happens and they have a fall, a first aid kit attached to the saddle may be unavailable just when it is needed most.

Leather bootlaces are another invaluable item to take with you because they are very strong and once tied they tend to stay tied. You can use one to mend just about anything. For example, if a horse treads on his reins and snaps his bridle, tie one end of the bootlace to the bit-ring. Now thread it up over the horse's head through whatever keepers and buckles remain of your bridle, holding it all in place and down to the other bit-ring. Adjust and tie off into the bit-ring. If you have a snapped stirrup-leather: whip a damp lace tightly over the two overlapping broken ends. Laces are also very good for tying your coat and extra gear to the D-rings of your saddle.

It is also a good idea to have a mobile phone with you, and of course you should carry some form of identification. An armband with medical details and emergency contact information is ideal.

You may also need:
- *Waterproof clothing.*
- *Maps for route.*
- *Compass.*
- *Horse brush and a sponge.*

- *Hoof pick.*
- *Food and drink for rider and lunchtime feed for horse if required.*
- *'Shoof' boot or similar.*

 And if you are camping out at night:

- *Tent.*
- *Sleeping bag.*
- *Change of clothing/dry clothing to sleep in.*
- *Basic toiletries.*
- *Cooking equipment.*
- *Food supplies for horse and rider.*

If you are planning your own trek where there are places to accommodate horses and riders, you will need to be sure that fencing is safe, that there is ample water available for your horse, and that feed can be provided by the establishment. If not, you will have to make prior arrangements for feed to be delivered. Even good doers will need a bit of energy replacement at the end of the day. If you are only out for a couple of days, it may be possible to carry a coarse-mix ration but it does add to the weight. When planning your riding day, a good average distance would be about 20 miles. Don't try to go too far. Leave yourself time to cover the miles you have planned. Break the riding up with stops for grazing (horses and riders), and spend time walking on foot to ease your muscles and your horse's back. A good lunch-stop where saddles can be removed and the horses given a chance to graze and roll will set you both up for the second half of your day's journey. You will find the ride more enjoyable if you vary the pace—a good walk, trot and a canter if packs and saddlebags stay steady. Unending walking is tiring and boring for everyone. Don't forget to look around you and appreciate the places where you ride. Common sense, good horsemanship and sensible planning will help to make your trek safe but still a journey of adventure.

## HINT

It is important to remember tack will need cleaning after being on the horse all day and numnahs and girths may need drying out or washing (and drying) before the next day. Perhaps you can use this as an opportunity to participate in your *Tack Cleaning* or *Saddlery Achievement Badges*.

Turnout doesn't need to be as formal as at a Rally or Branch Competition; younger Members in particular may appreciate the opportunity to dress their ponies up somewhat for the occasion.

# Branch Rides/Treks

A locally-organised Branch Ride that includes an overnight stop can be great fun. The best first step in planning a Branch Ride is to find a suitable place to spend the night, and then to work out the ride either side of it. The overnight venue needs space to accommodate horses: a mix of stabling and grazing might be the first choice but horses could alternatively be corralled behind electric fencing once they are accustomed to the system. Horses and ponies that get on with each other can be housed in a barn or yard overnight. It is a little like Pony Club camp.

There also needs to be somewhere for riders to sleep—a barn or a suitable space for tents to be pitched—and somewhere to eat. Some form of loo is needed, and also washing facilities: but it doesn't have

Accommodation facilities
can be quite basic.

to be sophisticated. Experience has shown that Members often prefer
it to be quite rustic (adult support riders and younger or very tired
Members could be driven back to their own beds for the night). As long
as Members can keep themselves clean enough not to cause offence
to their companions it should be OK. The evening meal could be a
barbecue or a fish and chip supper bought in. The joy of trekking is the
time spent with your friends and with your horse, so it is usually less
formal (and less expensive) than Pony Club camp.

Like camp, the Branch will need the backup of parents and friends
but a cross-country journey by horse, perhaps 40 or 50km to celebrate
a Branch anniversary or just a ride around the Branch boundary, is truly
great fun and a great learning opportunity. It can be a great experience
for all Members who enjoy a challenge, in the company of their horse
and of like minded friends.

# Glossary

*Achievement Badges* Awards given by The Pony Club for specific subject areas. Those considered most relevant for endurance riders are: Human First Aid; Equine First Aid; Care of the Foot; Countryside Access; Fitness; Road Rider and Map Reading.

*Aftercare* Looking after your mount after the ride.

*Arteries* Tubes or vessels which carry the blood from the heart round the body. By cooling the large arteries along the sides and down the hind legs you can cool the blood, and therefore the horse, during crewing.

*BioThane* Trade name of extremely strong webbing with a plastic coating.

*Bivvy bag* A sleeping type bag with good thermal and weather protection which can be used without a tent.

*Bum bag* A small bag or pouch on a belt worn round the waist to take essentials: e.g. first aid kit.

*Checkpoints* Points along the route where stewards (who are usually in contact with the ride HQ) check that you are safe and on the correct route. This is a safety measure to ensure that nobody gets lost.

*Chilling* This happens when the horse has become too cold too quickly through over-cooling. To compensate, his heart rate increases and he may visibly shiver. The efficient use of a stethoscope, to keep a check on the heart rate while cooling, can prevent this. A heart rate monitor (HRM) is even better.

*Competition Badges* Awards given by The Pony Club for specific disciplines. There are two levels for each discipline: the Intro badge and the Competition badge. These offer a good preparation for competition.

*CER (Competitive Endurance Ride)* Sometimes referred to as a 'gated endurance ride' or 'race ride'. For experienced, well-qualified riders only. Usually over 80km with a mass start. The first one home presenting sound with a heart rate of 64 or under is the winner. For any distance over 50km there is usually at least one vet gate or hold approximately 30 or 40km apart. You may present your horse as soon as possible with a heart rate under 64bpm, after which the clock is stopped and you may rest for anything from 20–40 minutes, depending on the rules of the day. The clock starts again at the time at which you should leave. This can be a tactical race and tends to be very competitive. Unfortunately different endurance bodies refer to classes and ride types by slightly different names. You should be careful to check the rules and class descriptions for the organising body of any event which you enter.

*Competitive Trail Ride (CTR)* See GER (Graded Endurance Ride).

*Contour lines* Lines marked on the Ordnance Survey maps, usually at 10-metre vertical intervals. The lines indicate the gradient of the land: e.g. the closer the lines the steeper the hill.

*Cooling* The major part of crewing can be the cooling of the horse to reduce his heart rate which is determined by the amount of energy he has expounded on the ride, creating heat. Cooling by sponging cold water on the main arteries near the surface: e.g down the hind legs, helps to bring the temperature down quickly. Other areas to cool are the neck, shoulders and belly. Wipe the water off as it becomes warmer, and keep up the process until you reach near the minimum heart rate required.

*Countryside Code* This is a code outlining how you should behave when in the countryside. One of the aims of The Pony Club in running endurance riding activities is to give young people and their families the opportunity to have fun and enjoy the countryside, and to promote environmental awareness.

*Crew/Crewing* The team behind the rider. Crewing is essential to the smooth riding and final presentation of the horse. Crews should ensure that everything is to hand when needed and that they have a cool head to cope with your rider!

*Dehydration* Condition caused by the loss of fluids and salts from the body, usually due to heat. It is a real problem with horses who won't drink enough water to replace the loss of fluids and salts through sweating during exercise. Cautious and correct use of electrolytes can help overcome this. Many horses willingly drink sugar beet water which has a natural source of energy. Riders can suffer dehydration too, and crews should make certain that their riders drink during the ride. Isotonic sports drinks help a lot.

*Dress* See The Pony Club's book *The Pony Club Pocket Guide to Equestrian Dress* for guidance. Each Branch of The Pony Club should ensure that its Members are aware of the requirements. However, dress at most endurance events (including Pony Club) is fairly casual. The correct standard headgear, recommended by the societies, along with correct riding footwear and comfortable clothing suitable for the discipline, with well-fitting tack for the horse, will suffice.

*Eagle* The fifth level of Pony Club rides: open category. 40–50km at a speed of between 8 and 15km/h.

*EGB* Endurance GB, the official body for England and Wales.

*Electrolytes* Electrolytes are referred to as 'tissue salts'. They are essential for the regulation of body fluids to prevent dehydration, and can be given to horses in water, gels, etc., to replace the salts lost through sweating during hard exercise. But they are a specialised product and should only be used as and when recommended: e.g they must only be given to a horse already drinking well and not to one who is refusing to drink.

*Energy* Energy is essential for the satisfactory completion of the ride by the horse and rider. It comes in the form of correct food and drink which is stored by the body and used up in relation to activity. Riders can use high-energy food bars and drinks to sustain them. High-energy feed for the horse should be used according to his temperament and the demands (i.e. distance travelled) made on his energy.

*Farrier* Your farrier is the endurance rider's best and most valued friend, taking care of your horse's feet and shoes for safe kilometres on the trail.

*Farriery Check* On most rides the condition of the horse's shoes are checked to see that they are safe and sound for the distance you are undertaking.

*Feed* The old saying 'feed according to work and temperament' holds good when you are working out requirements for endurance riding. Overfeeding can be just as dangerous as underfeeding. Knowing your particular horse's needs comes with experience. There is no substitute for good quality feed. Endurance horses need more forage (chop, hay) in the gut to retain moisture which in turn lessens the risk of dehydration; and a feed giving a slow release of energy.

*Fitness* The fitness of both you and your horse will make or break your ride. Both of you must be fit for the distance you are undertaking. Fitness in the horse can not be hurried, and hardening of the tendons and strengthening of muscles starts with boring walking not fast trotting. An unfit horse may well suffer strains and stress, leaving him unsuitable for future competition.

*Footwear* For Pony Club requirements see *The Pony Club Pocket Guide to Equestrian Dress*. Trainers and similar footwear (except specialist riding trainers which have heels and which allow you to run more safely alongside your horse) are never suitable for riding. However, if you choose to wear boots without a smooth sole, in order to offer more grip when you are on foot, then Pony Club rules are that you must have cages fitted to your stirrups. Long leather boots are not really suitable for endurance.

*Gait* The pace at which a horse travels. Walk, trot and canter are standard in Britain although some horses 'pace'—moving two legs on the same side instead of diagonally at the trot. If the horse has a naturally uneven gait you must mention it on your vet sheet (and hope that the vet accepts it as your horse's natural way of going and not as a sign of lameness!)

*Gated Ride* Usually used to refer to a ride which contains one or more vet holds or gates. These can be run either as GER-type or CER-type classes depending on the organising body and distance. The Pony Club Open Championships is a gated ride.

*Gates* The ability to unfasten and fasten a gate will speed up your ride. Generally the rule is that if you find a gate open then it is OK to leave it that way, if you find it closed then make sure that you fasten it securely behind you. N.B. Under some rules you may receive a 'gate allowance' if there are more than a certain number of gates on the route. This enables you still to ride at the designated speed set for that class: e.g if your riding time is to be two hours to ride at 10km/h and there is a gate allowance of five minutes you are allowed two hours five minutes to ride the course at 10km/h.

*GER* Graded Endurance Rides (sometimes known as Competitive Trail Rides) are rides where competitors are marked against a predetermined set of speed and heart rate criteria. All riders achieving this 'grade' receive the appropriate award. Such rides are not usually placed.

*Going* Good or bad going can describe the condition of the ground over which you are travelling. Good going might be grassy tracks, bad going may be stony, deep or wet ground.

*Golden Horseshoe* Famous two-day ride over Exmoor.

*GPS* Global Positioning System. The use of GPS devices is permitted under Pony Club Endurance rules: these devices are worn by the rider and monitor both location and speed.

*Grid reference* An Ordnance Survey map has lines going from south to north (known as 'northings') and from west to east ('eastings'). The lines have corresponding numbers marked at the side of the map going south to north and the line at the bottom going west to east. Read the eastings first (the numbers going west to east) then the northings (the numbers going from south to north). If you have trouble remembering which way round to read off the numbers, think of 'going along the hall and then up the stairs'. Where the two lines cross is the grid reference, which may be read as, say 670450. Each of the squares between the lines can be divided into ten. Supposing your point of reference is about halfway between 45 and 46 on the north/south line and a bit more on the east/west line—you could be more accurate and give the reference as 677455. A full-size Ordnance Survey map will provide all this information as well as a key to the symbols (called the 'Legend').

*Heart rate* The rate at which the heart beats. At rest it is usually between 35–45bpm. A rate of more than 64bpm on presentation to the vet at the end of the ride incurs elimination.

*Heart rate monitor (HRM)* Also referred to as a 'pulse monitor', this is used for keeping a check on the horse's heart rate while he is competing, and also at crewing. With a very small transmitter placed against the skin, either under the saddle or in the girth area, the heart rate can be detected and sent to a wristwatch type receiver which provides a constant, visible readout.

*Holds* Also known as 'vet gates'. A period of time during a long ride when there is a compulsory hold or rest-time for the horse.

*Hoof boots* Boots designed to fit around and under the hoof, protecting the foot in the absence of a shoe.

*Horsemanship* Endurance riding is a test of horsemanship: to be able to ride skilfully and with consideration for the horse, and by correct feeding and fittening, finish the ride in a condition 'fit to continue'. The Pony Club aims to promote a high standard of horsemanship, particularly in developing an awareness of fitness in both horse and rider.

*Hypothermia* A condition caused by severe chilling. The body temperature drops dangerously and the body slowly ceases to function. It can happen, for example, when horse and rider are not properly prepared for bad weather.

*ILDRA* Irish Long Distance Riding Association.

*In hand* Leading the horse from the ground with a bridle or headcollar is known as leading 'in hand'.

*Kestrel* The third level of Pony Club Rides: novice. 20–29km at a speed of between 8 and 15km/h.

*Log book* A folder issued by endurance societies (such as EGB, SERC and ILDRA) for storing records such as vet sheets, membership information, and the Master Card.

*Map case* You will need this clear plastic, waterproof case to hold your map and ride instructions so that you can easily refer to them during the ride. It is worn around the rider's neck.

*Markers* Signs or coloured tape (usually fluorescent), attached to a fence, tree, etc., to confirm your route, warning of a change of direction and indicating gates to be shut. Over open ground flags may be used. Lime powder or biodegradable spray paint are an alternative. The method to be used will be indicated on your ride instructions.

*Massage* Massage techniques can be used to relax the horse and thereby help to reduce the heart rate.

*Master Card* Your Master Card contains particulars of your horse and is a mileage record card. It is a safety net for the horse. Should your horse frequently fail through lameness, etc., the vet may advise you not to compete for a while. It records your horse's progress and provides a long-term record of his competition history and eligibility for higher level classes. You will not be allowed to start the ride without producing your Master Card.

*Merlin* The second level of Pony Club Rides: training. 10–19km at a maximum speed of 12km/h: no minimum speed.

*Neoprene* A soft rubber-type fabric used for boots and for covering a girth or breastplate.

*Number bib* All riders wear a number bib so that they can be identified at checkpoints etc.

*Obesity* Term used to describe fatness and being overweight.

*Ordnance Survey* The whole of Britain has been surveyed and mapped by the Ordnance Survey, who produce numbered maps for each area. These show all ground features: e.g roads, buildings, rivers—and indicate ground heights with contour lines at 10-metre vertical intervals.

*Osprey* The fourth level of Pony Club Rides: 30–40km to be ridden between 8 and 15km/h.

*Para-Endurance* Endurance rules and competitions aimed at making the sport accessible to disabled riders. Rides under 16km are organised by the RDA and over this by the relevant national endurance body.

*Passing* Always give adequate warning that you would like to pass other riders so that they can move over and you can pass in safety.

*Penalties* Depending on the organising body and class entered, in the final vetting you may receive penalties for bruising, over-reaching and soreness, as well as dehydration. Time penalties may also be incurred if you go below or above the optimum time for the particular ride.

*Performance Formula* A method of awarding placings in a GER-type ride. Also sometimes known as 'French' formula. (*See* page 129).

*Pinch test* By taking a pinch of skin on the horse's neck or shoulder and seeing how long the fold of skin takes to resume its normal state you can tell the amount of dehydration he is suffering. This is a usual part of the final vetting and may incur penalties.

*PR (Pleasure Ride)* Also known as a group, training or social ride. A ride of up to 40km, but usually a lot shorter, with a generous time allowance at maximum speed to protect the horse. Before and after the ride you are unlikely to have to do more than a 'trot up' rather than a vetting.

*Pulse* The measured beat or throb of the heart and arteries. It can be felt where an artery is near the surface of the skin: e.g under the jaw bone or behind the horse's elbow. Knowing how and where to feel and read a pulse on your horse can help you to judge his recovery rate. You should know his usual resting pulse rate. Using a stethoscope just behind his elbow on the near side will enable you to hear his heart rate.

*Quietness* A quiet, calm, unflustered crew will help a horse through his vetting more easily than a noisy, chaotic one.

*Quilty* Australia's famous long distance ride.

*Race Ride* A common term for the highest level of endurance rides (*see* CER).

*Ridgeway test* At the final vetting you horse's pulse rate will be taken. You will be asked to run the horse up in hand, and one minute later the pulse will be taken again. This will indicate the fitness and recovery rate of your horse. The pulse rate should drop on the second count on a fit horse and should increase on a tired one. It is also referred to as the 'Minute Test'. As it is not carried out in all endurance societies, check the rules.

*Riding time* Time taken to complete the ride but excluding any time at a compulsory hold or rest period.

*Robin* The first level of Pony Club Rides: training. Under 10km. Maximum speed 12km/h. No minimum speed. Suitable as an introduction for all members aged five years and over.

*Rugs* You will need a thermal-type rug that wicks away moisture while keeping the horse warm. If you use a sweat rug, put a light rug over it. For cold, wet days while waiting for final vetting, a New Zealand rug is a useful addition—particularly over the hind quarters, to stop muscles stiffening.

*SERC* Scottish Endurance Riding Club

*Saddles* Once you are competing in rides over 80km your GP saddle may not be suitable because of the pressures put on your horse's back from the length of time that you are on board and the miles covered. Thanks to new concepts in saddle design a variety of specialist saddles are available for the serious endurance rider. Whichever saddle you use, it must fit and be comfortable for both you and the horse. Remember that the horse will change shape with increase and decrease of fitness.

*Saddle sore (on horse)* A sore patch caused by an ill-fitting saddle or a foreign body: e.g. grit—between saddle and horse.

*Saddle sore (on rider)* A sore seat. A sheepskin or specialist seat-saver over your saddle can help prevent this. Good riding helps, too!

*Slosh* Water from a plastic bottle given by the crew, possibly on the run, to tip over the horse's neck and shoulders to cool him.

*Speed charts* *See* example on pages 62–63. These give you every distance from 1–80km; and the time and speed in miles per hour needed to cover that distance and are useful as a guide when you are working out projected riding times.

*Speed parameters* Minimum and maximum speeds between which you must complete the ride.

*Sponge* Essential equipment for crewing. Soaked in water it is used to cool the horse during and after the ride. Riders can also make use of any available natural water on the trail to cool the horse by carrying a sponge on a string clipped to their saddles.

*Spun* A term used to indicate that a horse has failed the veterinary examination.

*Start time* Time indicated on your ride instructions or vet sheet at which you must be ready to start your ride. In some competitions the clock is started at the stated time whether or not you are ready. Check the rules.

*Stethoscope* Used for listening to the horse's heartbeat by placing the diaphragm of the instrument against the horse's side just behind the elbow on the near side.

*Stress* This can be suffered by the horse in travelling to and from the ride; by the excitement of the event; by not being fit enough for the ride and having too little energy in reserve; or from not having sufficient liquid and becoming dehydrated.

*Sugar beet* A good addition to the feed. Soaked beet pulp helps the horse's gut to retain fluid by damping down the feed. Beet pulp water contains a little sugar and can boost energy levels if offered during and after a ride.

*Swellings* After a ride it is quite possible for your horse to have slightly swollen joints. Bandaging or the use of cooling packs, followed the next day by gentle exercise, usually reduces these swellings. If they are on the back they may be caused by poorly fitting saddles or bad riding.

*Sweating* The horse will sweat when working, excited, hot or stressed. Salts and body fluids are lost by sweating and need to be replaced to reduce dehydration. Some horses sweat more than others.

*Talkround* Also referred to as 'Ride Instructions'. These written instructions correspond to the route marked on your map.

*Terrain* The type of ground over which you are riding. It could be very steep, rocky or boggy, and you would have to ride at a slower than average pace. You may be given a 'Terrain Allowance' if the organisers think that you will have difficulty in making the maximum time allowed.

*Tevis* Reputedly the hardest 100-mile-in-one-day event in the world and a forerunner of today's great endurance rides. Organised by the American Endurance Rides Conference.

*Timekeeper* Official at the start and finish clocking you out and in, keeping a record of your time so that award/speed can be worked out.

*Trot up* Pleasure riders will probably only have to 'trot up' their horses for the vet before and after the ride rather than having a full vetting and may be allowed to present the horse tacked up. Check the rules.

*Tying-up* This condition is also known as azoturia or 'Monday morning sickness'. It is usually brought on by too much stress too soon in the ride, with a sudden build-up of lactic acid in the muscles, producing intense cramp. The acid build-up may be caused by too high protein food being retained in the horse's system.

*Vaccination* At some big rides, or where horses are to be stabled overnight or starting on racecourses, etc., it may be compulsory for your horse to have an up-to-date vaccination certificate.

*Vet gate* See 'Holds'.

*Vet sheet* At most rides you are likely to have a vet sheet. This will show details of your horse's age, height, sex etc., and will give you your vet time and a start time. It will also ask for any injuries or peculiarities of gait that you want to bring to the vet's attention. The vet will in turn record comments to as a reminder of the horse's condition for when they, or another vet, see him at the finish; the horse's starting and finishing heart rate; and also whether he has completed or failed the ride. Keep a copy for your records.

*Vetted out* Term used to describe failing the veterinary examination before, during or after the event. Your horse may be vetted out before the ride if the vet does not think him sound or fit enough to compete. At a vet hold or at the end of the ride the horse must be sound, with a heart rate of 64 or under, or he will be vetted out or 'spun'.

*Venue* The place from where the ride starts.

# Contact Details

**The Pony Club**
Stoneleigh Park
Kenilworth
Warwickshire
CV8 2RW
Telephone: 02476 698300
Email: enquiries@pcuk.org
Website: www.pcuk.org

**Endurance GB**
Telephone: 02476 697929
Email: enquiries@endurancegb.co.uk
Website: www.endurancegb.co.uk

**Scottish Endurance Riding Club**
Email: info@scottishendurance.com
Website: www.scottishendurance.com

**Irish Long Distance Riding Association**
Email: webmaster@enduranceridingireland.com
Website: www.enduranceridingireland.com

**Riding for the Disabled Association**
Telephone: 0845 6581082
Email: info@rda.org.uk
Website: www.rda.org.uk

**The British Horse Society**
Telephone: 02476 840500
Email: enquiry@bhs.org.uk
Website: www.bhs.org.uk

# Photography Credits

The Pony Club would like to thank the following photographers for their permission to use the photographs as listed below:

© 2011 *Rexphotography* Front cover

© 2014 *Aaron Gallavan* Pages 59 (top), 60 (bottom-left), 68–69, 72, 80, 88, 103, 132–133, 139

© 2014 *Barbara Baker* Pages 84–85

© 2014 *Barbara Wigley* Page 11

© 2014 *Carri Ann Dark, Dark Studios* Pages 12–13

© 2014 *James Smillie & Chris Teagles (www.ct-photo.co.uk)* 60 (top-left), 60 (bottom-right), 61 (left), 61 (right), 110–111

© 2014 *Jane Alexander* Page 135 (top)

© 2014 *Jon Lee* Pages 18–19, 60 (top-right), 70, 109, 113, 117, 122

© 2014 *Jo Sinar, Starzphotos* 42–43

© 2014 *Nicola Parsler* Pages 14–15, 21 (top), 21 (middle), 21 (bottom), 22 (top), 22 (bottom), 25, 28, 30, 31 (top), 31 (bottom), 32, 33, 34–35, 45, 52–53, 59 (bottom), 66, 67, 74, 76, 87, 94 (top), 94 (bottom), 98–99, 101, 104, 107, 124, 126, 137, 142, 143 (top), 143 (bottom-left), 143 (bottom-right)

© 2014 *Rebecca Parsler* Pages 134, 135 (bottom)

© 2014 *Rosemary Hogarth* Pages 8–9

© 2014 *The Pony Club* Pages 24, 65

© 2014 *West End Photography* Page 39